Superconscious Relationships

The Simple Psychic Truths
of Perfectly Satisfying
Connections

(This Is Not Your Parents' Relationship Manual!)

Superconscious Relationships

The Simple Psychic Truths
of Perfectly Satisfying
Connections

(This Is Not Your Parents' Relationship Manual!)

Margaret Ruth

BOOKS

Winchester, UK
Washington, USA

First published by O-Books, 2010
O Books is an imprint of John Hunt Publishing Ltd., The Bothy, Deershot Lodge, Park Lane, Ropley,
Hants, SO24 0BE, UK
office1@o-books.net
www.o-books.com

For distributor details and how to order please visit the 'Ordering' section on our website.

Text copyright Margaret Ruth 2009

ISBN: 978 1 84694 458 1

Design: Stuart Davies
Illustrations: Jud Laird

Printed in the UK by CPI Antony Rowe
Printed in the USA by Offset Paperback Mfrs, Inc

We operate a distinctive and ethical publishing philosophy in all
areas of its business, from its global network of authors to
production and worldwide distribution.

CONTENTS

Chapter 1   Hello and the Easy Place to Start   1

Chapter 2   Cut the Crap   13

Chapter 3   The Immutable Law of 100–0   28

Chapter 4   Find What You Want To Have, Be and Do   49

Chapter 5   Only Three Things   66

Chapter 6   Thing 1: Tune In, Tune Up   82

Chapter 7   Thing 2: What Music You Play   103

Chapter 8   And Thing 3 is Not Your Job   119

Chapter 9   Then Flip It for Thing 3*   137

Chapter 10   Find Fabulous New Things about You
             Using Mirrors   151

Chapter 11   Put It All Together – It Works   165

Chapter 12   A Clear New Reality Plus Bonus
             Refrigerator Door Material   173

Chapter 13   Good Bye for Now   187

Acknowledgements   190

With humor and love, the inimitable Margaret Ruth comforts, cajoles, and kicks our butt as she lays down the closest thing I've seen to The Truth: that the locus of power lies in each of us, and why let it lie fallow? Read this book with a highlighter. And then read it again and again, until you "get it." It's that good.

Greta DeJong, Publisher and Editor of the 28 year old *Catalyst Magazine: Healthy Living, Healthy Planet*

Great answers, right to the point, and very empowering. Superconscious Relationships is timeless in showing how to get to the bottom-line of healthy, satisfying relationships; yet remains relatable to the Millennial Generation. It shows you how to love yourself, and how to give and receive equally in a relationship by cutting through cultural clutter. By far the best relationship book I've ever read.

Zack Shutt, Author of the Millenial Generation breakthrough novel *Blogs of Wrath*

Margaret Ruth has an uncanny ability to get to the bottom of relationship problems. But what really sets her apart is her solid, practical, and effective advice about how to solve them.

Christy Karras, Journalist and Author of *More than Petticoats: Remarkable Women of Utah*

Margaret Ruth's newest book Superconscious Relationships is a valuable read for anybody, regardless of his or her relationship status. Whether you are happily married or desperately looking for your next romantic encounter, the most important point she clearly illustrates is that all of us can always improve the most relationship of all: our relationship with ourselves. In reading through her easy-to-understand chapters, you will inevitably run into a personal epiphany or two about what you can do to be happier and attract healthier relationships in your life.

Yumi Sakugawa, Editor of the premier wellbeing website Intent.com

Real and practical guidelines for successful relationships. Instead of merely offering advice, Margaret Ruth challenges young readers to look at themselves, encouraging us to take responsibility and control over our own internal landscapes. Within the text there are also a number of helpful exercises that improve our abilities to create genuine, superconscious relationships. Whether you're a metaphysical maestro or a self-help skeptic, this book is invaluable.

Erin Rosa, Journalist and past Associate Editor of *Campus Progress*

This Book is Dedicated to Two Great Men

John Laird Hensler and **James Bennett Hensler**

Pith Helmets Optional

Chapter 1

Hello and the Easy Place to Start

Typical, average and usual relationships are *not perfect* for you. If they were, you wouldn't be reading this book. – Margaret Ruth

The young radio caller's voice broke. "Margaret Ruth," he asked me, "When am I going to have real relationships? Nothing ever works out for me."

Why hasn't the available psychological, physical and metaphysical advice helped us have better relationships after all this time? Why does trying to connect with family, friends and partners still feel so difficult? What does it take to experience real relationship satisfaction? The direct answer is that it doesn't take much — if what you want is deeply satisfying and fulfilling personal connections with others.

If that is your goal, realize that what you want is perfectly possible and be relieved to know that it is very simple too. We are going to cut through cultural clutter and persistent relationship myths to clarify exactly what is necessary for happier experiences with the people in your life.

There are just a handful of basic, immutable truths about how authentic human connections develop and once you grasp these underlying metaphysical truths, you and your relationships will never be the same. You will enjoy meaningful, personally enriching bonds that are right for you, for the rest of your life.

Be Perfectly Happy in Relationships

I have heard the sincerely affecting personal stories of thousands of radio callers and clients as a professional psychic and metaphysical teacher; it is probably not surprising that relationship anguish is the number one problem. Wanting to know how to have rewarding, satisfying connections with others is a recurring and constant need.

A client of mine, Lisa, had come to her psychic reading fully prepared, carrying a notebook, a back-up recorder and extra recording tape. She was frantic for better relationships, declaring: "I've done a lot of letting go, and I know I take on people's issues too much and have stopped doing that. But, people still have to realize that Lisa hurts! It is hard for me to trust, hard to be close to people, unless they can think of what I am going through." Lisa was taken aback when I showed how her declaration actually prohibited healthy connections.

Then there was Anthony, whose plummeting self esteem and growing loneliness from being single at 36 made him panic: "Margaret Ruth, I am willing to compromise! At my age, you can't be picky." "Anthony," the mean old psychic told him, "this willingness to compromise in your relationships is a clear pointer to your real problem."

Many people, like Lisa and Anthony, remain unsure and insecure about their personal connections. Commonly expressed concerns are similar to these:

I work so hard at my relationships, why aren't they better?
I always date problem people – what is wrong with me?
I always give and give and never seem to get it back.
My mother-in-law makes me so mad – she doesn't appreciate me.
Why can't I fit in with the others?
I always feel worn out by my co-workers' problems – should I quit my job?
This relationship is a roller coaster – will it always be like this?
All I want is for people to listen to me and they never do.

My girlfriend never seems happy with me.

I have terrible fights with (_fill in the blank_) that ever get resolved.

I never feel like I have good friends.

By the end of this book, you will be able to answer these questions yourself. My direct answers and simple insights into solving these specific issues are summed up in Chapter 12, so you don't have to figure out all of it on your own (*and I know, because I'm psychic, that some of you cheaters are looking ahead right now*).

Younger Adults Know to Find the Easy Zip-Tab Solutions

This is a not-infrequent comment around my house: "Mom, what is your problem with ripping bags open? There was a zip open tab with an *Open Here* sign right on it." Apparently, a part of my 50+ year old self is still living in the Stone Ages of packaging and thinks that bags of printer paper, salads, chips, and peat moss need to be torn apart to access the contents.

It seems that the younger a person is, the more habitual it is to look for the easy-open tab to get what is wanted. This is good news, because you youthful (and youthful thinking) adults are open to the clarity of this book's model of personal connections. By wanting to go directly to the essential building blocks of meaningful relationships, you can cut through an array of extraneous and unnecessary information. This book is like the zip tab that just gets the

job done – because it is going to be very simple – and I need you to accept that.

We older types struggle with these easy-open solutions and seem to want, or be used to, complications and exceptions. It is odd but true that I can almost estimate someone's age by how many *except-whens, what-abouts* and *don't-forgets* that a person wants to slather onto the few concepts of this book. These impulses to add decorative items, and in some cases add things that don't make any sense at all, make it hard for us to absorb a simple framework like the one presented here. But, if you are in your twenties or thirties, you will have this advantage on us and be able to readily enjoy how really clear it can be.

ISSUE BOX

I have a question, Margaret Ruth
If it is all very simple, why would it take 200 pages to explain?

MR: Good question. It will only take a few pages to describe the five piece framework of perfectly satisfying connections. I have found that you complex readers easily understand the simplicity of what you must do to have authentic relationships – so that is good so far. But then you all have trouble getting your entire multi-layered self, and your old habits, and old assumptions, and old notions, and old relationship memories, aligned in one straight, clear direction. The book's remainder is therefore addressed to the more complicated problem: you.

This is all right with me, however, because if you were not so complex, you wouldn't be asking these hard questions (like, "HOW do I get my relationship act together?"). And then we would not have met.

An Easy Place to Start: The Single Best Working Assumption for Drama-Free Relationships

> We also often add to our pain and suffering by being overly sensitive, over-reacting to minor things, and sometimes taking things too personally. - Tenzin Gyatso

I want to immediately explain a simple, non-psychic, handy idea that can immediately remove – starting today – about 10% of the usual relationship angst from your daily life.

Now, and tomorrow, and always, assume that the person you are relating with is doing the best s/he can for that particular time and that specific situation. No matter what others are doing, have this thought ready: *"That person is giving me her or his best available response – for this situation and this moment,"* and you will start feeling better about relationships and other people instantly.

There are several reasons to make this your ongoing working assumption.

Good Reason #1: Accuracy

First, this assumption is accurate roughly 85% of the time. The odds are very strong that at any point in time, what you are getting from another is the best that person has, for that moment, for that situation. Few people are going to go out of their way to undermine their relationship with you.

Read this next sentence a couple of times: Taking something upsetting personally implies that the other is consciously trying to hurt your feelings. That motivation is relatively rare. It occurs sometimes but, if it is the case that someone wants to hurt you deliberately, why closely associate with such a person? Keep those folks at a distance.

On the other hand, sure, there are times when someone is consciously not giving you her or his best. But, most of the time, what you are seeing or hearing from others is what they can manage at that moment and they are usually not making a deliberate attempt to upset you. Attempting, with clear intention, to make another miserable usually requires more energy than most people want to expend.

Good Reason #2: Avoiding Emotional Quicksand

Making this thought your default assumption keeps you from possible emotional-quicksand pits generated when two people's inner anxieties, troubles and frustrations start rubbing against each other. This happens quite frequently when people are not consciously processing. Picture yourself in this example scenario where the following internal dialog occurs in you and the other who is bugging you:

Your Inner Angst Generator: Boy, that guy gave me such a brush off. He must not think well of me or not care about me. I know he could do better so therefore he is deliberately hurting me by not giving me better behavior. I am angry – that person gave me a bad reaction! I am ripped off! I am hurt! That person is bad!

Meanwhile…

The Other Person's Inner Angst Generator: I am so stressed...Life is getting me down...I can't cope...

Labeling other people's reactions to you as "good to me" or "bad to me" allows you to take everything someone does personally. You can get trapped in allowing other people's bad moods to affect your well-being – all in the name of a personal affront.

It gets more complicated the closer the tie. Imagine that your significant other does something that upsets you. You could start fuming or getting mad: "How dare she treat me like that!" But, really, *what is going on with that individual* is what is dictating her behavior, and not what is going on with you. You might provide a catalyst for her reaction through a word, look or deed, but it ends there.

You are going to be much happier if you start thinking, "Ok, I did not like that, but I am assuming that was the best she had for that moment and this situation." You can try to have a healthier give-and-take about it later. Or, if this type of inter-action is frequent and continues to be unsatisfying, you can re-think your part in the relationship in general. More on that below.

Good Reason #3: Being a Happier You

The last reason to carry the handy working assumption with you is that when you are not taking other people's stuff personally, you maintain your perspective; call it a healthy perspective. In cultivating an understanding that, most of the time, most people are giving you their best available, you can start looking at which relationships are worth sustaining.

Here is an example. You care about punctuality but have a friend who is absolutely never on time. You explain your wants. You beg. You communicate. You sulk. Nothing works; she seems to go out of her way (she must be!) to disregard your feelings and be late. You start getting angry. You know she could change her behavior if she cared! She is a wretched human being to treat you like that!

But, if you would choose to assume that what she is giving you is really the best she has in this area, then you can make a decision. Knowing what you are getting is her limit – it does not get better and it is not personal – now what do you want to do? There are many choices available and none of them any better or worse than the other; all that matters is what you want. Keep the relationship as it is, now that you know she won't ever be punctual? Downgrade it to casual friend level? End the relationship with mutual understanding?

Whatever action you pursue from this more informed perspective, you are guaranteed the situation is going to become much healthier for all concerned, without the current level of relationship frustration.

Last Discussion Bits

Vocabulary Words

> We can't define anything precisely. If we attempt to, we get into that paralysis of thought that comes to philosophers... one saying to the other: "you don't know what you are talking about!" The second one says: "what do you mean by *talking*? What do you mean by *you*? What do you mean by *know*?" – Richard Feynman

It is very helpful to know what speakers or writers mean when they use words that have several definitions. Two speakers may be describing a very similar idea and yet use two different sets of words, or vocabulary, to convey their thoughts. Therefore, it is good to be flexible with each other in our vocabulary requirements. Communication between people seems to flow best when we do not require others to use our set-words in their own expressions.

And yet, it will be helpful to clarify for you how I am using some of the book's terms. So, for this bit of writing in front of you, here are my words that may need explanation.

Metaphysical – My use of the word metaphysical refers to information and concepts that transcend the three dimensional and five-sense physical boundaries; these are ideas that cannot be identified or quantified using physical measures. For instance, the conception of human consciousness as a separate thing from the physical body is *metaphysical* because we cannot physically prove yet this condition exists, although some people's personal experiences might say that this is a valid perception.

Whole – A person who could be described as Self-fulfilled, Self-integrated and Self-assured (it sounds great, doesn't it?). I am using this word to point to a person who would have qualities such as a fully integrated inner self, well defined persona, solid positive sense of self and without a need for anyone else to complete it. Whole means being self-fulfilled and self protective.

Healthy – A willingness to feel great: physically, mentally, emotionally, and spiritually. I am using healthy to denote more than sound physical health. Healthy, in my usage, describes choices that do not diminish or hurt the individual in any physical, mental, emotional or spiritual way and, in addition, choices that help the individual grow in these areas.

True – In this book, true means authentic and valid for you and your experience. The word *true* is often used in a more scientific way to indicate things that are factual and can be proved by observation to be accurate. This is handy because I will show you how your observations of your and others' life experiences will verify the concepts we discuss. So, you can verify that they are personally and logically *true*.

Assumptions – This word is related to words like *notion, preconception, and belief.* It is something that you suppose to be true. For instance, by purchasing this book, you assumed, or made an *assumption*, that Margaret Ruth might be able to write well enough for the reader (you) to understand her points. As I have gotten this far without a grammatical or punctuation error, your *assumption* might prove to be correct.

Model – This is a representation, like a blueprint of a building or a sculpture that depicts an idea or thing. The model we build in *Superconscious Relationships* is not only a representation what holds great relationships together, but it also gives a road map, another kind of model, that shows how to get to the goal.

Work – is a four letter word here because its connotation of excessive effort and difficulty make it ineligible for use in describing how to develop a healthy self and healthy relationships. For purposes of this book, *work* is something that is draining, difficult and feels like drudgery. The words *maintenance, effort, play* and *focus* will be used in lieu of work to indicate times when you give something your attention.

Shorthand Notations

HJW stands for Healthy Joyful Whole and is a short notation that indicates how we want to feel about ourselves and our relationships.

EEE stands for Even Energy Exchange. It is a concept that is valid not only in metaphysical frameworks, but also in the more academic areas of economics and business. It implies that all transactions must eventually balance out somehow, whether physically, mentally, emotionally or spiritually.

> **This book focuses on close, in-person, voluntary, social and adult relationships such as good friendships, romantic partners and life mates**.
>
> There are, though, many types of possible connections such as: impersonal, distant, acquaintance, business, casual, electronic, just for fun, club, web forum, Facebook,

convenience, occasional, intermittent, mixed, dating, married, professional, forced, geographic, or proximate.

Many of us have in-person, social relationships that are somewhat non-voluntary, meaning that we did not exactly get to choose these people like we did friends and spouses. Family, in-laws or neighbors are examples. Some of these can become quite close and spending time together might be perfectly voluntary.

Then there are also impersonal relationships, which arise for business or professional reasons. Contacts such as visiting a doctor, making a sales call, standing at the cashier, or sitting next to another student, are largely impersonal.

And Next

And there you have all the preliminaries. The next project is to begin dismantling the prevailing relationship falsehoods that you and I have been absorbing throughout our lives and get rid of them. My secret psychic tool for this? It's called the Scientific Method.

Key Points Summary

Superconscious Relationships will cut through a vast array of relationship information to get to the bottom line: simple metaphysical truths of authentic, fulfilling relationships.

The book's focus is on adult, in-person, close, voluntary, social relationships.

Relationship problems are pervasive and yet are also highly

individual. The underlying concepts we examine can help you solve yours.

The complex problem is the multifaceted *You*. It takes an entire book to help unwind from of old assumptions, beliefs, ideas and self concepts.

I find that the younger generation of adults easily understands a plain, direct and clear relationship model. The older a person is, the harder it is to accept how simple it can be.

Get some immediate relief from relationship-induced botheration by carrying handy assumption #1 around in your back pocket. Assume that other people are giving you the best they have available for the time and the situation. It will be correct *most* of the time and it will keep you from having to take everybody's behavior personally. You'll be instantly happier.

We went over my particular vocabulary words and abbreviations.

Thank you, by the way, for deciding to peek at this book. I am glad to meet you.

Chapter 2

Cut the Crap

Everybody gets so much information all day long that they lose their common sense. – Gertrude Stein

Reading for Bethany psychically reminded me of scrambled eggs. Her reaction to a divorce was a flood of conflicting thoughts, emotions, beliefs and nagging questions: "What did I do wrong? Why is he doing this do me? Should I have tried harder? Will I always have miserable marriages? What is the healthiest next step? What revenge is most painful?" It was hard to find Bethany under all that.

The natural place to start is with You and your current state of relationship ideas, beliefs and attitudes. Most people are a mixed bag of these, so it's understandable that when it comes to relationship issues, most people are mixed up. They are surrounded by contradictory examples, models and information. This outside input often differs from their inner feelings, desires and beliefs. You and I can experience information overload from outside our selves and from within.

Therefore, we want to find out how to get rid of relationship ideas that do not actually work and relationship beliefs that are not actually true. We also want to find out how to only accept information that will help us improve our relationships and our lives.

A Case of Too Much Relationship Information

I want to start with an illustration of someone experiencing a serious relationship crises; it attempts to show how an overabundance of inner and outer chatter is overwhelming.

Can you see yourself, perhaps just a little, in this? I know I can, and I think we can also recognize the constant patter of inner dialog that accompanies us through an upset. We all have a level of inner processing that is not only our thoughts, but also our beliefs, ideas, assumptions, habits, training and attitudes. It is so constant that we hardly notice it at times. At other times, it is like there are several champion college debate teams duking it out in there, using our inner landscape as a stage.

Notice the overpowering glut of input from friends, family and culture; our picture is a realistic representation of that experience for many of us. From our handy working assumption, we can be fairly sure that the people talking to this upset woman are trying to give the best response they have for the situation and time. Some might even be giving her good information, but how do we know the good from the bad?

Taking Steps to Leave Relationship Trauma Behind

In a situation where you or someone you know feels as conflicted and torn as shown here, the very best first step is to start meeting with psychological, healing and spiritual counselors. Often, these can help a person stabilize. It is very difficult, if not impossible, to work with the material in this book and relationships if you do not feel physically, emotionally or mentally well. *Let good people use their professional training to get you started in a healthy direction.*

Here is the point of examining this scene. Information overload like this is not good when it has negative consequences such as confusion, inner conflicts, emotional paralysis, feelings of instability or mixed efforts. If the overload generates distressing results, we know the person involved is not being helped by it.

Exercise: Visualize a *Prime You*

As we think in our hearts, so we are. – Proverbs, 23:7

The opposite of all the above is when a person feels centered, calm and clear on what is best for him or her. We all want to aim for this but getting to that state can seem impossible. Like the person in the illustration, if we are not aware of the multiple layers of our internal dialog, we have a problem.

Additionally, how much or what kind of information from other sources should you and I absorb? If we make ourselves available to all the opinions of others, books, dogmas, or even vastly gifted and insightful psychics like Margaret Ruth, we will be overwhelmed and confused. I am not sure if any counselor or healing professional would recommend that you absorb everything ever thrown at you and be content with the inner turmoil as a way of life.

Often when I am doing a psychic reading for someone, it turns out that she or he cannot fathom what it might feel like to be clear and centered. Many cannot even imagine themselves as whole, perfectly self aware and impervious to unhelpful opinions. People want to know, "What does all that *centered inner harmony* stuff even *mean*??"

The next tool is a *Metaphysical Magnifying Glass*, one that spotlights a possible ideal energetic map of you so you can get a sense of what to aim for.

Metaphysical Magnifying Glass

Metaphysically, aim for a You, with a capital *Y*, that can process all the inner and outer information clearly, easily, and effectively. This *Prime You* has a calm and secure center, plenty of self enriched layers, a helpful input processing sorter, a bad information disposal outlet and a semi-porous, bounce-back outer layer.

Start by picturing yourself as a multilayered and multifaceted composition. You could think of your multi-dimensional self as a symphony, a recipe, a garden or work of art. Know that every single dimension and part of you contributes to the vibrational information that you throw off. You could envision this as your *vibe, vibrational signature, aura, field* or *greater spirit*. These types of shorthand names refer to your nonphysical imprint.

Take a Metaphysical Magnifying Glass and go closer. Now picture your personal field as a sphere of energy.

ISSUE BOX

Hold On Margaret Ruth

What does it mean to picture myself as a "sphere of energy" or whatever you are writing here? I mean, I am Me. I see myself in the mirror. That is Me. What exactly are you talking about?

Recall that my use of the word metaphysical refers to information and concepts that transcend the three dimensional and five-sense physical boundaries. You are more that just a physical being. You have a unique consciousness, meaning that your individual spirit animates your body and this consciousness, or spirit, is more than just the physical part we all see.

To be able to encompass this expanded notion of your Self, I want you to relax into a picture of the entire system of You – one that is your physical self and expanded by a larger ball of energy that is your vibe, aura or spirit that you give off and carry around with you. So, in essence, I want you to think of You as more than just what you see in the mirror.

If I could pick, your magnifying glass would reveal the following layers. The *Prime You* has a semi-porous, non-breakable, bounce-back boundary; this relates to what psychologists term "having good boundaries." Having a personal boundary allows you to understand what feelings, energies, problems, thoughts, ideas and sensations are yours. Acquiring one enables you to discern then what of these also belong to others. This boundary also has a filter.

Visualize the filter part of the boundary in your mind. No one else's stuff can get through without going through the filter;

therefore you are not absorbing other people's word or emotions or thoughts as your own. This filter admits only beneficial ideas, thoughts, opinions and images.

Prime You has a clear, unobstructed, untainted calm center core in the middle. Think of it as the nucleus of a cell or a no-color egg yolk. The ideal is to have the center feel light, energetic, secure, perfectly round, whole, and undented. There would be no confusion, no tensions, nor anybody else's stuff there. This crystal clear center represents your essential self – the core you. It contains the spark of your individual spirit and the connection to the larger field of energy that illuminates, enlivens, and animates your consciousness.

Then, between the clear center core and the filter boundary are your self enrichment layers. These layers are developed as you go about living your physical life. Self development layers are created by such things as your hobbies, ideas, experiences, travels, books, pets, books by Margaret Ruth, and your relationships. Your assignment is to grow and expand those layers as wide and as far and as long and as rich as you can.

And I always think it is nice to add a *Bad Information Disposal and Discharge Outlet* too.

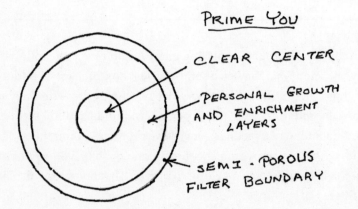

PRIME YOU

CLEAR CENTER

PERSONAL GROWTH AND ENRICHMENT LAYERS

SEMI - POROUS FILTER BOUNDARY

All of this is one way to envision a *Prime You*, one that only allows in positive input and never allows anyone or anything to muck around with your essential core.

Picture of Blob Sort of Self

This inner nature is not strong and overpowering and unmistakable...It is weak and delicate and subtle and easily overcome by habit, cultural pressure, and wrong attitudes toward it. – Abraham Maslow

Quite a few people look something like this picture, kind of like scrambled eggs.

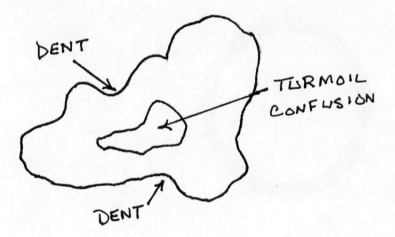

In our blob-self picture, others' ideas, of what the person should think, do and be, have infiltrated past the weak filter boundary and into the core of the individual. This sort of imploded and dented energetic self implies factors like lack of trust and love for the core self as well as bad boundaries – a problem that psychologists warn us about. This is a picture of allowing other people's ideas and impressions to reach in and interfere with the center of the inner self.

If you and I don't develop a good boundary and filter, an appreciation for our essential self, and enough personal development layers, we are going to feel like the picture.

I really do not want you to feel like this picture.

Picture of Steel Shell Person

Some people do not let ANYTHING in. An impenetrable shell keeps fresh air, new views, creative insights, as well as other people's feelings and ideas out and therefore there is no growth. Often the Steel Shell people don't seem to get rid of anything either, so I find them mostly recycling old ideas or their fondest notions – over and over again.

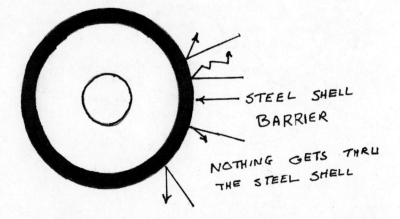

STEEL SHELL
BARRIER

NOTHING GETS THRU
THE STEEL SHELL

It is difficult to a have perfectly fulfilling relationships with rigidity.

Exercise: Picturing a Clear Center

This is a simple meditation and visualization exercise that can help you start becoming more aware of what is going on inside you.

Take a moment to close your eyes and use your inner senses to visualize your whole self as a sphere of projecting energy. This sphere of your self has a center. You might want to visualize this center around your navel area.

Keeping your eyes closed, sense what your center looks like. What shape is it? What is in there? Do you sense colors, shapes, vibrations, sounds perhaps? Fully explore your center.

If you are having trouble sensing this center part of you, do not worry. Try asking it questions if you are stuck. Ask it to show itself. If you cannot see it in your inner eye, ask it to tell you about itself. Then allow words and images and sounds to come through. Don't edit or push. Let it be a simple, flowing sort of conversation.

Trust what you get. If you see colors, or knots, or breakage, know that these all have a meaning. The words or sounds you might get convey meaning.

Take it another step if you can. Once you get an idea of what might be going on in your core self, superimpose a visualization that makes you feel calm, such as picturing a bright, clear, serene globe of energy in the middle of you.

Ask yourself to answer questions such as: How far away am I from this picture? What can I do to have this as my day to day inner reality? Are there any blocks or knots appearing in this center? Again, don't edit or push, but allow yourself to get thoughts, ideas and feelings about this.

The more you try to picture your clear center, the easier it gets. Use your intuition to make it even more personally effective by adding your own details and ideas.

Start Sorting, the Scientific Method, and Stating What is Actually True about Relationships

"The exception proves that the rule is wrong." That is the principle of science. If there is an exception to any rule, and if it can be proved by observation, that rule is wrong. – Richard Feynman

Our inner beliefs, which often spawn from untrue but often repeated relationship ideas and assumptions from outside of us, often feel true. The next best step is to start de-cluttering by dissecting these to identify stuff that is true as well as stuff that isn't. One effective sorting tool is the scientific method: *If you can find just one exception to a statement, then the statement is not true.*

The scientific method is accurate and efficient for testing statements that we either hold inside already or hear from others. A notion or idea can seem true for *some* people *sometimes*. However, if there is any exception then we know for a fact that it is not really true because it doesn't occur all the time, under all conditions.

Once you can sort and debunk erroneous concepts using insights from this book, personal observation, logic and the scientific method, it is crucial that you replace them with statements that are *actually true*. I cannot emphasize enough how important replacing old ideas is; so make sure this always gets done.

To demonstrate how to restate falsehoods into actual and true statements, I am going to start by testing some commonly held beliefs and some of the most pervasive and damaging notions surrounding romantic relationships (since these particularly bug me) and restating them to reflect truth.

Debunk the Four Worst Relationship Falsehoods

Horrible Relationship Myth #1: *You Complete Me*

Or, in other words: "Falling in love makes a person whole." "If I love you enough, you will feel better." "If you love me enough, I will feel better." This implies that a person cannot feel whole without another loving them.

This is completely misguided. Does it make logical sense that we must be loved by others in order to feel complete? This is very bad news for loners and single people.

What is true is that some people benefit from the support and assistance of someone who loves them. On the other hand, because there are many counterexamples of individuals who never seem to get or feel better - no matter how much they are loved and assisted - we know that loving someone does not automatically help get them happier or healthier.

What is also true is that the more complete and whole we are, the better our connections with others. The causal arrow runs that way: first we are healthy, and then we have healthy relationships. First, we are happy, and then we have happy relationships. See *The Missing Piece Meets the Big O* by Shel Silverstein for the definitive word on this topic.

This misstatement then can be restated into this true statement: *No one can complete another; however love and support can be beneficial.*

Horrible Relationship Myth #2: *Relationships Take (Exhausting) Work*

The truth of the above statement hinges on what the speaker

means by the word *work*. Some relationships have trouble running smoothly. Mediocre relationships often need some drudgery to keep them going. These are like bad cars that keep breaking down and need constant repair.

Sure, yes, the vast majority of people, especially those of my own Boomer Generation, have less than fabulous relationships that require a certain amount of laborious effort to maintain. And these folks want to tell you that this is normal! *"Relationships Take Work!"* usually translates to: In order to keep many relationships going, you have to do a lot of pushing, and repairing, and ignoring, and...

On the other hand, there plenty of wonderful, happy, healthy connections that do not take grinding amounts of toil to keep them running – they only take attention and maintenance. So, if the word *work* in the statement implies drudgery and exhausting toil, then the statement is false. If the word *work* means paying attention and applying effort toward positive maintenance and upkeep, then it is true.

So, what's really true is: *Healthy, joyful relationships take attention and effort to keep them running well, not exhausting toil and arduous drudgery. If a relationship is constantly breaking down, that is not ok just because it is "normal."*

Horrible Relationship Myth #3: *Relationships Require Compromises*

If you are currently in or are contemplating a relationship that requires you to sacrifice or compromise something important to you, you do not have a perfectly happy or healthy relationship. Excellent, healthy relationships do not require any kind of a major compromise on the part of either person.

People use this myth as an excuse to accept less than what they really want in their important voluntary relationships – like romances – in order to feel seemingly safe. No one however has ever been made emotionally or mentally safe by compromising what s/he really wanted or negating essential aspects of the self.

What is true is that great relationships seem to thrive on cooperation. These often exhibit the spirit of mutual support, vision and teamwork. People who care for you, the authentic you, will not ask you to compromise who you are and what is important to you to make them happy.

What is really true: *Relationships seem to thrive on cooperation, but someone who loves the authentic you will never ask you to compromise important parts of yourself.*

Horrible Relationship Myth #4: *No One is Perfect*

This has many guises: "No relationship is perfect," "It's unrealistic to expect a perfect relationship," and the worst, "Since I'm not perfect, I won't get/deserve a perfect relationship or a perfect partner/friend."

Many of us were taught to believe that our permanent life-job is to fix our virtually uncountable personal flaws. These insidious flaws are shown to us constantly on air brushed magazine covers, advertising and television. And apparently these flaws keep others from wanting to befriend us, date us, or – and this is the most frightening – mate with us.

I know that I have gotten to the point where I have to ignore all American network television shows and women's magazines (and I do mean ALL) so not to get depressed and start wanting to frantically locate flaws to fix.

What is true, metaphysically, is that there is some flawed person out there that could very well be **perfect for you**. There are men and women out there who do not look like magazine models, aren't millionaires yet and have zero athletic trophies to their name and still they could be wonderful possible mates because of their attitudes, personalities or adorable smiles. They are perfect in the way they fit the type of relationship that you enjoy.

The other good news is that you, despite never having been on a magazine cover, could be perfect for them.

True Restatement: *There are people out there who are perfect friends, buddies, and mates for you, and you for them.*

And Next

If some of the popularly held ideas about interpersonal connections are not true, then why do we hear them so much? Why does *everybody* insist that involvements are difficult and complicated? What is the one false assumption that creates so much drama and problems in the usual types of relationships?

I am going to next begin building a relationship framework that reveals how the general level of confusion about human connections persists and why, in truth, it is all really simple.

Key Points Summary

When trying to figure out relationship problems, many people will be overwhelmed not only by all of the information thrown at them from the outside, but also by their own inner dialog occurring at all levels of self

Reaching for the healthiest options can involve setting appointments with well trained professionals to get started in feeling better as soon as possible.

A visualization of a *Prime You* and an exercise on focusing on your center were covered, and to which I hope you will add elements and adjust to make them specifically helpful for you.

- Metaphysically, the aim is for a You with
- a calm, clear and inviolate center

- as many self enrichment layers as possible
- an effective input processing sorter
- a bad information disposal outlet
- a semi-porous, bounce-back, non-breakable outer layer whose filter only allows positive and helpful data to enter

One very potent and easy tool for sorting and determining what is really true about relationships is a scientific method where the exception disproves the rule. If you can find just one exception to some oft-repeated tale of how relationships work, then you know it isn't completely true.

We did some myth-busting and then determined these following statements are actually true.

No one can complete another; however love and support can be beneficial and appreciated.

Healthy, joyful connections only take attention and effort; if there is arduous work involved and a relationship is constantly breaking down, that is not ok just because it is "normal."

Relationships seem to thrive on cooperation, but someone who loves the authentic you will never ask you to compromise important parts of yourself.

There are people who can be perfect mates, friends and buddies for you, and you can be perfect for them.

Some Further Good Reads

The World According to Mister Rogers: Important Things to Remember by Fred Rogers

The Missing Piece Meets the Big O by Shel Silverstein

Chapter 3

The Immutable Law of 100–0

While we may not be able to control all that happens to us, we can control what happens inside us. – Benjamin Franklin

Help Margaret Ruth! My husband is making me miserable. I ask him. I beg him. I nag him. He ignores everything. He's ruining our relationship!

There is a basic and immutable truth that governs human consciousness.

Many of you will recognize my statement of it as similar to those of numerous other metaphysical writers and teachers. It additionally parallels concepts from philosophy, physics and psychology. Fully understanding it allows you to make perfect sense of your relationship experiences and this book.

What I have found is that some of us – for instance: *me* – need an easy and handy catchphrase for remembering this foundational principle; so mine is The Hundred-Zero Law or, in short, 100-0 Law.

Part I: The Law

The 100-0 Law

The 100-0 Law is that every human adult on the planet is 100% responsible for, and has 100% control of, her or his internal landscape. It might sound very strange to you, but it is actually good news. Each individual is ultimately the only one who can make the choice as to the condition, conduct and content of this inner personal realm; this includes thoughts, feelings, reactions, beliefs, assumptions, ideas, memories, self talk, information processing and, well, absolutely everything else.

Because the 100-0 Law is true, then so are its two corollaries. First: No other person has any more impact, influence, control nor responsibility for our internal conditions than we allow. In other words, without our permission – conscious or unconscious – to influence us, others have 0% control, influence, or responsibility for our internal conditions.

Second: Conversely then, we have 0% impact, influence, control or responsibility for any other human's inner universe. Without their permission, we cannot affect these at all. At some level, we allow each other – anywhere from a little, to a lot, to none whatsoever – power to influence our inner universe.

Does this Law make sense to you? If you already get it – good.

Perhaps the Law seems novel, or contradictory, or confusing. This chapter is devoted to comprehending how it and its extensions affect you and your personal involvements. Because of the Law's importance, I will want you to verify it for yourself so that you are absolutely certain that it is the operating system protocol for us human types

This is a Weird Law, Margaret Ruth – Not Many People Follow It

"But the Emperor has nothing on at all!" cried the little child.

– Hans Christian Andersen

The 100-0 Law applies to everybody all the time. Otherwise it wouldn't be much of a Universal Law. It would be a rather measly and wimpy not-very-universal sort of law. It does however hold true whether or not individuals believe it, understand it, go with it or work against it.

What happens is that many people act as if there is a different law in place. We often see people behave and speak as if others had enormous control, and even responsibility, for their feelings, happiness and beliefs. You and I hear statements like the following all the time:

My husband is driving me nuts
She made me upset
He made me so happy
You are making me sick
My boss stresses me out

Our cultures instill in us, from an early age, that we are responsible for others' happiness with messages like: *Make your coach proud. We'd all be happier if you tried to be nice. Stop making the teacher so upset. You kids are hurting your mother.*

And if we are able to impact others' well-being, then it must also be the case that others affect our own. Therefore, our kids are driving us crazy, the politicians are ruining our mood, our spouse is causing us stress and our neighbors are making us mad. But none of these impressions are true since no one can make us feel or think anything without our conscious or unconscious cooperation.

Plus, living our life not understanding the 100-0 Law is hazardous to our health; believing otherwise means that everyone on the planet has the power to make us unhappy, which, of course, is something *they* are constantly going to continue to do into the permanent foreseeable future without cessation or pause.

In contrast, the Law says you get to pick how you feel. It is a Good Law.

Despite the Universal Truth of the 100-0 Law, It Doesn't Get Much Press

The 100-0 Law is a foundational principle for understanding interpersonal relations; it however contrasts with two conventional, and equally opposing, conceptual paradigms. Trying to describe both of these in a general sense does them no justice, but it does enable me to lump mainstream modes of thought into two basic categories. So, here then is my lumping.

The first paradigm is that an individual's life experiences are dictated either somewhat or completely from the outside via a higher authority such as __(*insert here denominational or non-denominational Creator/Goddess/God Force of Your Choice*)__. The job of a human is to obey and/or appease this outside force so that things go well. And – if things do not go well for our example human – s/he is to just take it and hope that upon death a much nicer place, __(*insert here denominational or non-denominational nirvana/heaven/afterlife of Your Choice*)__, awaits with all the rewards earned in this particular lifetime. We could loosely call this an authoritarian construct where we are required to do as we are told or follow the guidelines in order to be ok.

The general idea of the second category is *determinism*, a mechanical view of cause and effect. It posits that forces that affect humans can be objectively studied and measured. It is scientific and causal – personal events are determined by body conditions, social conditions, weather conditions or initial conditions. In a completely deterministic model, people are often reactors to the various conditions and stimuli imposed upon them. I have no incentive to wade into the centuries-old *Free Will versus Determinism* debate right now, but as you can imagine most metaphysical frameworks, such as the one in this book (where individuals are more than just their physical bodies) fall decidedly on the side of *Free Will*.

These two viewpoints can be pretty persuasive, because it means that individuals can use other sources than themselves to be certain. People like certainty. We like to be sure. If you use the scientific approach, rules can be *proved*. If you use a perfectly authoritarian approach, instructions can be *conveyed*.

In both these frameworks, what is happening with people's inner self may not always be under their control because it can be affected by outside forces and events. Thus, these two causal constructs, or set of assumptions, tend to imply something rather different than the 100-0 Law.

Be Conscious Today

Your worst enemy cannot harm you as much as your own thoughts, unguarded. – *Dhammapada: The Sayings of Buddha*

What makes 100-0 so hard for some people to comprehend is that reactions, which are at some level a function of personal choice, *feel* like they are not chosen at all.

We are actually always choosing on some inner level our responses, but when we are not conscious of this inner processing, acting from indoctrination and habit seems unavoidable. Choosing reactions consciously will unquestionably raise the awareness level of your important relationships. You start becoming superconscious and you can start doing this today.

One helpful step is to watch what you are saying out loud or thinking internally. Catch anything that implies someone else controls your thoughts, feelings and reactions. Stop immediately and change to a statement that is really true.

Here are examples of how to do this by replacing untrue statements with some new true statements:

True: I have confused feelings over something my husband did
     instead of *My husband is driving me nuts*

True: I am upsetting myself over what she said
     instead of *She made me upset*

True: I really let myself feel happy over what he did
     instead of *He made me so happy*

True: I am making myself feel sick about this
     instead of *You are making me sick*

True: I stress me out over this
     instead of *My boss stresses me out*

For some people, this exercise drags them right out of their comfort zone. However, it has to get done even if there is kicking and screaming involved because there is nothing healthier for you than acting and speaking truthfully.

So, get good at it – if you like the idea of taking good care of yourself.

Not making others in charge of your reactions also has a side benefit. They will appreciate it! People will be relieved of that particular burden when you understand that it is actually you who controls your own feelings.

ISSUE BOX

Margaret Ruth, this 100-0 is really hard to accept!
A part of me is really resisting. My mind says the 100-0 Law is correct. My gut is pushing against because it scares me. I find myself wanting to keep the option of blaming others for how I feel. It seems so hard to take all that responsibility solely on myself. However much my mind, and my wiser self, understands the 100-0 Law, my fears and old training, I guess, are fighting it.

A part of *me* is extremely sympathetic to how this is stirring up old stuff in your inner landscape. Feeling inner conflict when faced with a new and contradictory realization is pretty reasonable and natural.

Another part of me wants to say: *"Hey, the faster you get that old internal stuff to stop kicking up a rumpus in there, the better.* You and I both know that to continue for the rest of your life acting *as if* others can impact your psyche, and acting *as if* they even had some responsibility for it, is to sentence yourself to a very long future of less-than-perfectly-satisfying relations with others. So, if you truly want extraordinarily satisfying connections, eventually all parts of you need to, as my father used to insist, "Get with the program." Since it is just a matter of time before you bring all of you into an acceptance and understanding of the 100-0 Law, I say the sooner, the better.

And – just think of how happy everyone else is going to be when relieved of responsibility for the contents and conditions of your inner universe.

But, then again, the resistance and inner conflicts that you are experiencing are normal and not strange at all. Try affirming statements like these: *Although I allowed past*

> *events and people to affect me, I am choosing to not let them to affect me any more. I have let ideas, events and people from the past control how I feel, but I can choose to feel differently from now on. Only I can choose what I let affect me from now on. Nothing, including my past, can affect me other than I allow.*
>
> See if those help, or see if you can generate some that are even more effective, and let me know what you come up with!

Verify the 100-0 Law for Yourself

When we actually begin to realize that we can control only our own behavior, we immediately start to redefine our personal freedom and find, in many instances, that we have much more freedom than we realize. - William Glasser

A potent substantiation of the 100-0 Law is the fact that humans demonstrate the ability to profoundly and radically change old unhealthy attitudes, patterns and thoughts. We've all seen this happen in instances where someone chose to seek out new ideas and beliefs, and felt better as a result. Perhaps they undertook successful psychotherapy, studied a spiritual path, traveled to exotic cultures or pursued alternative avenues of self help.

When people choose actions such as these and then come to feel or believe differently, they prove that cultural indoctrination, outside influences and ingrained personal habits do not have to be permanently retained in the inner psyche.

A thought experiment demonstrates something we constantly observe in reality, which is that identical stimuli or situations fail to cause a consistent reaction among individuals or even within your self. Sit quietly for a moment and then, one at a time, imagine you are participating in these two scenes.

Scene 1: Visualize being at a workplace with some co-workers.

A voice on the speaker loudly says: "You're too slow!" Ask yourself how you feel and what you would think if that happened. Further imagine that each person there has a different reaction. One might get fearful about job security. Another may ask for advice on how to do better. Another may be completely calm and mutter, "Ignore that."

Here are questions for you: *What is your reaction to the others not agreeing with you or acting as you do? Is the variety of people's responses to the same event possible or realistic in your opinion?*

If it seems feasible to you that everyone exhibits different behaviors although provoked by identical outside stimuli, then you know that individuals must be able to choose their inner reactions – as opposed to inner reactions being forced upon them by the outer event. To the extent that someone can choose to process disembodied criticism, like *You're too slow,* as a personal affront, or choose to completely ignore it, depends upon that individual's internal processing.

Scene 2: Picture that you and I are chatting and strolling down a crowded city sidewalk. Someone loudly says, "You're too slow!" Now, check with yourself and get the sense for how you would react to that. *Do you get upset? Feel hurt? Roll your eyes and forget about it? Does it ruin your day? Not bother you at all?*

Most people say they react differently to what is the same comment, with the same content and in the same delivery, as the earlier one. It is the same stimuli exactly but the receiver usually gives each a different association depending upon the context. "The context is what leads to the association, so it was the setting context that created the responses," is what one scientifically minded, brilliant young man argued (my son Laird). But, distill it further.

This is a case where the recipient and stimulus were identical, and so only the setting was different. Since other associations and interpretations ARE available in that setting, then at some level, these processes are completely subjective. The only one who had any control over the response was the one doing the relative associating and interpreting. In your case, that one would be You.

And associations that have become ingrained can become un-ingrained.

And here is further evidence of the 100-0 Law. Reflect on your own life and past difficult relationships. No matter how hard you tried (as a matter of fact, you probably even "worked" at it) to get others to be happy or love themselves, many of them never did it. If you really had any control over them, they would've been happy – because that's what you would have picked for them to feel if you had been the actual inner-landscape-controller. There are only two alternatives to explain this failure: either you never had any control over their psyche at all or you were really lousy at controlling their happiness. Either way – you are fired.

The corollary is that no matter how hard others tried, they also failed to make you perfectly happy. Perhaps then they never actually had perfect influence on how you felt after all.

Let's take a moment, forgive everyone, including ourselves, involved in attempting the impossible in the past and move forward by finally recognizing the actual operative governing formula is the Law of 100-0.

Part II: Don't Break the Law

Even Energy Exchange

> If you begin by sacrificing yourself to those you love, you will end by hating those to whom you have sacrificed yourself.
>
> – George Bernard Shaw

The 100-0 Law implies that healthy and voluntary adult friend-ships must be mutually beneficial, or they will not continue. This is because each individual is 100% responsible for their personal well-being and will not remain in a situation that does not support that. The Law of Even Energy Exchange, or EEE, is an extension of this and it states: *Mutual emotional, mental, physical and energetic exchanges must be roughly even in some way in order for all parties to be satisfied enough to sustain the relationship in any healthy kind of manner.*

The key concept here is balanced reciprocity. People refer to this as getting as much giving. It can get tricky though to identify what exactly the participants are getting from their affiliations. What we give in voluntary social interactions is more than our money; it is our time, our attention, our mind, our energy, our hearts.

It is hard to maintain a mutual connection without some even exchange of some sort over the long term. Ultimately, some member of an *un*balanced involvement will consciously or unconsciously do something to bring it back into balance such as back away, get angry, change the existing dynamic, or pull a stunt.

One of the more surprising results of the EEE Law is that, more often than not, the persons appearing to be receiving more than they are giving are the ones to eventually break the connection. The Givers of the broken relationship, *who gave the other everything!* experience shock and meltdown when the Taker flakes. I see this all the time in my job doing psychic readings for people.

This is counter logical until we understand EEE. At some level, usually unconsciously, everyone involved is aware of the energetic imbalance and something has to happen, as these systems cannot be maintained as they are. Rarely do you see a conscious awareness of all this though;

---

if people were fully aware, they would do something consciously to fix the exchange imbalance.

As it is you will find, littered all over the psychic landscape, the carcasses of care-giver/care-getter relationships where the Taker had to take off for some random, sudden and typically not very logical reason.

Testing for EEE and 100-0

There is a quick way to tell if a relationship operates with EEE: Do the people involved seem happy and healthy? Don't ask them if they like their relationships. Plenty of people will claim to like their relationships, despite the fact that these connections appear draining, exhausting or upsetting. So, asking won't work. Instead look to see if the individuals seem upbeat, joyful, energetic, peaceful or otherwise positive when around each other.

What if you don't get those impressions about your friendships? If they violate either Law, the 100-0 or EEE, there are ways to test for it.

If you are taking on more than you are supposed to in a relationship, a useful keyword is *drained*. In these cases you could feel worn out, exhausted, over worked, tired, weary, put out, nervous, tense, anxious, worried, critical, dissatisfied, rejected, unacknowledged or unappreciated. Those feelings *can* indicate that you are making yourself responsible for something that doesn't belong to you – either the other's feelings or for their half of the connection.

There is the converse to the above. If someone is giving more to a relationship than you are, or if you are not holding up your end, or if you are allowing someone to carry your feelings and worries for you, the keyword is *resistant*.

You might feel the following: strained, restrained, inhibited, withholding, numb, resentful, defiant, rebellious, disdainful, uncaring, uninvolved, indignant, passive, detached, disinterested, dull, reactive or manipulated. And if all those sound like being a teenager, there is good reason for it.

Recognize the Real Boundaries: You Are 100% Responsible for You and 50% Responsible for the Relationship

In adult, voluntary, personal involvements, the two Laws of EEE and 100-0 dictate that you are responsible for holding up your share – and only your share. You are 100% responsible for your well-being. You are 50% responsible for your half of the relationship's well-being. You are 0% responsible for the other's inner landscape and 0% responsible for the upkeep of his or her half of the partnership. Don't mess with these boundaries; failure to keep them results in relationships that are less than healthy, satisfying and rewarding.

I use *adult, voluntary* and *personal* for a specific reason. Being careful to only be in charge of your half does not apply to cases where you are acting as a parent, healer, helper or caretaker – either in a professional or volunteer capacity. These are tasks that imply a different association that that of close friend or partner.

If someone becomes another's caregiver, the line between personal connection and job can blur.

A nurse I know was trying for a while to assist her ailing mother. She quickly became frazzled, quipping that she had UEE (Unbalanced Energy Exchange) when the mother-patient cantankerously refused to do everything possible to heal. My friend couldn't quite separate familial daughter feelings from volunteer nursing task. Every time her mother balked, she felt it as a personal loss.

Many avoid trying to heal loved ones because of the natural

difficulty of enmeshed boundaries, but then turn around do it anyway because they love them too much to not try to help. It is a tricky balance to pull off.

What you cannot do

You cannot decide what the others are going to do with their 50%, nor force them to do what you want them to do with it. You can try to set a role model for healthy relationships. You can try to encourage them. But, in the end only they can decide what to do with their half.

If they aren't holding up their end, you cannot accuse them of damaging your inner self or your half of the bond, because they cannot damage your psyche and they are not responsible for your 50%. They can only damage themselves and their half of the relationship.

What you can do

You can commit to handling your half in the best way you can manage. You can decide that you will hold up your 50% by becoming the most healthy, whole person you can be; this is what you have 100% control over. You can decide, and only if you want this, that one way you want to take care of your half is to be available to others with advice, guidance or help. However, you cannot make anyone accept your offers of support.

You can observe if the other 50% of your relationship is being taken care of in a healthy manner by the other, over the long run. If it isn't, even after all that good role modeling, and cajoling, and pep talking, and begging, and therapy – and everything else you threw at it – you can decide what to do with your 50%. If you see that the other end is not being handled in a way that makes the relationship worthwhile to you after all that, you can drop your half by taking a few steps back or even ending the entire relationship if that is the healthiest thing to choose.

There is some confusion over what taking care of one's 50% requires.

One persistent notion is that partners need to make the other happy. Since in actuality no one can make another happy, operating a relationship under an imperative of making the other happy is doomed-doomed-doomed, as no one will actually become happy under that regimen.

There are also plenty of people who think that they must carry more than their share in order to be a good friend, partner – or worse – to be a good person. But, this thinking just causes problems because of EEE. For someone to continually take on more than half is to become an unpaid therapist which in turn sets up a victim/martyr or a caretaker/dependent dynamic.

Please cut to the bottom line and take my word for it that these particular dynamics have never led to wonderful, superconscious, perfectly satisfying adult connections.

Common Critiques

Passengers should be advised to don their own oxygen masks before assisting others with their masks. – American Federal Aviation Administration Advisory Circular

Critiques to the material in this chapter, and to my observation that boundaries must be firm in order to support the best kind of relationships, mostly fret about the enormous emphasis on the self that the 100-0 Law requires. These criticisms sound good but do not, upon closer inspection, make too much sense.

Frequent Critique #1: *This emphasis on one's self encourages self-absorption and selfishness.*

This critique is sort of silly because it is hard to imagine the world being better off when individuals remain unfulfilled, unhappy or unhealthy. It is in all of our best interests to promote self-awareness and fulfillment for as many individuals as possible.

It seems unlikely that *you* finding out what is best for you is an event that diminishes *me*. Perhaps some of the people closest to you may be disrupted by your new found self-interest; otherwise, for the rest of us, you being a whole and complete person is now, and always will be, very, very good.

Note too that selfishness is best defined as you doing something for yourself without thinking of me. But, you are not in charge of me, I am. I get to think of me and you get to think of you. Those are the actual job assignments and so do not let all of this whining about how selfish you are confuse you.

Frequent Critique #2: *These self-fulfillment, self-emphasis programs take attention away from larger social issues and contributions to community affairs.*

The underlying assumption for this kind of critique is the fear that if individuals are allowed to be self-referring and self-interested, they will mostly fall into greed, hoarding, intolerance and other anti-social behaviors. These people will disregard the needs of their communities and cease to care about the welfare of others.

This is an interesting perspective on human nature. It seems that a portion of the world believes that humans are inherently bad and another portion believes them to be inherently good. I do not imagine that we can convince the portion that believes that humans need to be prodded into charitable and community concerns to change its mind, so I won't even try.

If individuals like you are reaching to be as healthy, joyful and whole as possible, it seems unlikely that compassion and sympathy will be lost in that particular process. What is the chance of those who are focusing on that kind of positive personal fulfillment will all of a sudden develop a bunch of fear-based traits, such as greed?

Both of these arguments start looking bizarre when viewed in the big picture. The entire world benefits every time someone takes care of his or her self as that is one less person who needs extra assistance. This allows more resources to go to those who cannot do this yet. Taking good care of yourself is one of the least selfish things you can do.

What This Means

The message of Existentialism...is about as simple as can be. It is that every one of us, as an individual, is responsible—responsible for what we do, responsible for who we are, responsible for the way we face and deal with the world, responsible, ultimately, for the way the world is. – Katharena Eiermann

If the 100-0 Law is true (and it is), it further reveals something very important. We now know that it is up to only ourselves to create our sense of happiness, inner peace and all of the good stuff – because no one else can do it for us. If we care for ourselves, we are then taken care of. If we love ourselves, we are then loved. Although we can certainly give others permission to influence us in these areas, in the end, we must do it for ourselves.

It means that we cannot wait for others to get their acts together, sign the right laws, end the wrong fights and – watch out – *complete us* before becoming healthy, joyful and whole. To be 100% responsible for our internal conditions is to no longer have any excuse. This realization allows us to take the time and energy needed to spend it with ourselves. Once you grasp the 100-0 Law, you know that you must now do your own inner journey towards self awareness. You become the explorer of that vast, wild, untamed terrain of You.

I have a nice pith helmet you can borrow.

Self Help *(This is a Personal Growth Book After All)*

Stop for a moment to ask some crucial questions. Are you committed to caring for your own self first? Are there parts of you resisting, not really sure you can achieve, or even deserve, happiness? Are you comfortable with letting go of any disabling patterns? Is it hard to visualize yourself as a happy, healthy, whole person?

Put this book down until you can do these. You will need to be able to clearly see yourself healthy and whole or you will get mixed results. Your efforts will reflect only what you can picture and thus come short. There is no way around it. And there are no exceptions. The magic comes from acquiring a firm view of a positive future self and feeling perfectly comfortable with a You that is very happy, very healthy and very satisfied.

Key Points Summary

Here is a summary of the entire Law and what it means for you:

The 100-0 Law Every adult person is 100% responsible for and has 100% control of the condition of his or her inner landscape. Therefore, you have 100% choice on what goes on inside yourself.

Corollary 1: Others have 0% control of, influence over, or responsibility for anyone else's internal condition. No one can impact your internal well-being and condition without your permission.

Corollary 2: You have 0% responsibility for, influence over, or control of others' inner landscape. Without their permission, you cannot impact them at all.

This is the operative law – no matter what - whether or not people believe it, know it or understand it

Correctly interpreting relationship information now and for your entire future requires the basic understanding that your personal reactions have little to do with the others involved.

Others cannot *make* you feel, react or think in any way. They have 0% control over your inner processing and feelings and, unless you give them permission, their stuff cannot provoke you at all.

You have no impact on or responsibility for what others choose to think or feel. Unless they allow it, you cannot influence them at all.

You can start watching your personal reactions and language, and change statements that violate the 100-0 Law into some that are true.

You can verify the 100-0 Law by observing the different reactions that you and the people around you have to the same stimuli, under various conditions.

The Law of Even Energy Exchange is an extension of the 100-0 Law and it says – for voluntary, close bonds – that emotional, mental, physical and energetic exchanges must be roughly even in some way in order for all parties to be satisfied enough to sustain the relationship in any healthy kind of manner.

The boundaries are thus clear: you are 100% responsible for your well-being and 50% responsible for the relationship's well-being. You are 0% responsible for the other's inner condition and 0% responsible for the upkeep of their half of the partnership.

For someone to continually take on more than their half in a personal relationship is to set up either a victim/martyr or a caretaker/dependent dynamic. Please take my word for it and avoid them because these particular dynamics, in settings other than parental or professional, have never led to superconscious, life enhancing connections.

Critiques mostly fret about the enormous emphasis on the self that the 100-0 Law dictates. These criticisms sound good but, upon closer looks, do not make too much sense.

We all must create for ourselves our sense of happiness, our inner peace, and all of the good stuff – because no one else can give it to us or do it for us.

Taking care of yourself is therefore your primary concern. Attending to the well-being of your self, your life and your individual consciousness is crucial and the whole point of being a human with this individual consciousness.

Your doing this is best for everybody else.

Some Good Further Reads

The End of Certainty by Ilya Prigogine (Note from MR: You can skip the math parts if you choose and still get the main points)

Taking the Quantum Leap: The New Physics for Nonscientists by Fred A. Wolf

The Holographic Universe by Michael Talbot

*Choice Theory: A New Psychology of Personal Freedo*m by William Glasser

Chapter 4

Find What You Want To Have, Be and Do

This process of the good life is not, I am convinced, a life for the faint-hearted. It involves the stretching and growing of becoming more and more of one's potentialities. It involves the courage to be. It means launching oneself fully into the stream of life. – Carl Rogers

Tina wrote me: Tell your readers Margaret Ruth that drama does not equate to a healthy partnership. The real thing has no drama and yet is incredibly fulfilling. Comparing old paltry dating experiences to my amazingly rich and meaningful marriage says it all. It took us quite some time to find each other, but we're happy that we didn't settle for second best. As diverse as our interests are, our personalities really resonate with each other. We each found the best person for us.

Have you ever been so hungry that you dove into whatever was available in the fridge: withered beans, congealed gravy, cold rice? Your initial hunger was minimally filled, but there might have been little satisfaction and possibly some unpleasantness at the end.

There is a similarity between reaching for whatever is available to sooth your hunger and that of being so empty that you feel you have no choice in your relationships. Both suggest that the trade-off between immediate satiation and fulfilling enrichment is not really worth it in the long run. If you reach for just whatever is available, you will not get exactly what you want.

Ultimately, because the 100-0 Law is true, people who have an enormous need for others to fill them up will never feel satisfied with their connections and blame it on others. Conversely, if you know how to develop the fullest and richest whole you, you will readily generate personal relationships that match how you feel about you.

Building a Model for Superconscious Relationships

The blueprint for generating perfectly satisfying connections that we are assembling is complete, comprehensible and, what is more, parallels what many spiritual, psychological and metaphysical teachers have prescribed. It also makes perfect logical and common sense when viewed overall. I like it.

The base of the superconscious relationship framework, or model, that we are constructing is the immutable 100-0 Law that governs our inner experiences and dictates how conscious inter-personal connections develop. Upon that base, the chapter after this one builds a three-sided prism that entirely describes how to generate genuine bonds with others.

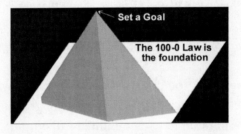

Our Initial Relationship Framework

To be able to build our model, you next decide what you want, because your desires set the direction for everything else. Not knowing exactly what to aim for is like acquiring a roadmap of the wrong destination. The model diagram here indicates that we only need the base understanding of the 100-0 Law and your personal goals in order to know what to construct next.

ISSUE BOX

Complaint Margaret Ruth

You say you are going to build a simple model of superconscious relationships that is comprehensive, logical and parallels other fields of study. This absolutely cannot be; it is inconceivable that all that can be contained in the model you describe. There must be more to it than you suggest.

No, actually, it is simple (not easy, but simple). And, I now know the questioner here is about my age, too, as we older folks just have to have all the bells and whistles of complications and add-ons. I refer you back to Chapter 1, younger adults, and the Easy Zip Tab Openers.

So. What Do You Want?

Reflect on traits that describe your ideal relationship experience. What do *you* like best about your personal interactions with companions, friends and partners? Words that come first to me are: *warm, expansive, sharing, real* and *laughing*.

You might conjure up the image of a relationship where you feel understood, there is mutual regard, there is a lot of fun involved and both people are happy. Most people find being appreciated for who they are makes a bond not only easy, but also fulfilling. Other qualities of wonderful connections can be *joy, satisfying, fun, open, evolving, trusting, serene, inspiring, supportive, understanding, authentic, rewarding, equal* and *healthy*.

And to this list, you have to add your own terms and concepts. Ask yourself, if you were in a perfect – for you – friendship or romance, what would it be like? How would you feel? What words would describe it? What are you and the other doing to make the close connection so appealing?

Make sure you notice and write down what comes up (*go ahead – jot right in the margin here – yes, right now*). Do not edit yourself; do not argue with yourself; do not hold back from fully expressing what you want.

This is important.

There are too many options, when it comes to selecting what your future experiences will be like, for you not to be fully conscious about setting your aim. Without deciding what you do want, and sticking to it, it is too easy to fall back on mythical rationalizations: *Relationships are hard! No relationship is perfect!* It is too easy to slide back into the regular and usual patterns that typify the majority of people's connections. If that happens, you will turn around in six months' time and proclaim that since your relationships remain difficult and unsatisfying, then Margaret Ruth is The Dumbest Writer on Earth.

And, well. I don't want you to do that.

You must choose. To not choose, or to compromise your real wishes, is to keep your status quo. You must acknowledge that you want something better if you want this change in your life. Set the dial to what is the best for you, move towards that standard and do not look back.

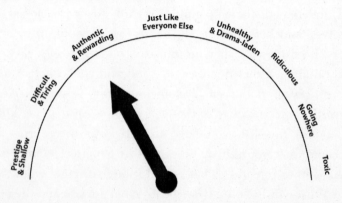

This Book's Goal is Then HJW Relationships (and No Other)

Typical, average, normal and usual relationships are *not perfect* for you. If they were, you wouldn't be reading this book. Our working assumption will be then that we want to enjoy healthy, joyful, whole (HJW) experiences in our close friendships, romances and partnerships. I choose these words to encompass some possible ideals discussed earlier such as mutual growth, acceptance, authenticity, healthy choices, enrichment, good boundaries, balance and happy feelings.

Meeting these objectives only requires grasping the basic metaphysical laws that govern how people connect and then substituting these for any ingrained bad habits and erroneous beliefs. We've already covered the 100-0 Law and its extensions, like the Law of EEE, and there aren't many more left to go.

Notice though, if you are not aiming for all that, this book won't help you; the remainder of it explains how to experience only HJW bonds with others. It doesn't need to address anything less than perfectly satisfying ones because there are plenty of authorities writing on how to manage and cope with difficult, exhausting, drama-laden, "you need to make me happy" relationships. You and I are talking about something quite a bit different in this book.

Do These Wonderful Relationships Exist?

> Where there is love there are no demands, no expectations, no dependency. I do not demand that you make me happy; my happiness does not lie in you. If you were to leave me, I will not feel sorry for myself; I enjoy your company immensely, but I do not cling. – Anthony de Mello

You are dutifully reading this chapter and have become *willing* to *begin* believing that extraordinary relationships exist. It is hard though, because, if they do, you have not really seen one. And, then, you might have noticed some, but you have never yourself been in one. As a matter of fact, you are pretty sure you haven't even met anyone who would match the qualities of HJW relationships.

So, this whole "setting our aims and goals" thing is sort of, you know, vague. Pie in the sky. Unrealistic. It does not feel tangible, doable or possible. There is a disconnect between a comprehension of these written words and your actual life experience.

I recently met with Greg, who asked about falling in love one day. It was a tough subject for him. He was brought up in very typical circumstances and had therefore developed a belief that marriages are difficult, imperfect, full of compromises and, thus, requiring a fair amount of drudgery to maintain. His past experiences had verified all these beliefs.

He was startled to hear me emphatically state that great, low drama, warm and perfect bonds exist, and that anyone who wants them can have them – if they choose it. This was completely new information for him. He was comforted and he was relieved. For him, there had been too many trips to bars with too many buddies full of advice on how to pick up women: how to act, what to wear and how to talk.

How miraculous it was for Greg to find out that some people have fulfilling, enriching, satisfying and authentic relationships: *You have a decision, Greg. You can decide to have the usual type of marriage, or you can decide to join the joyful, healthy, whole segment of the population, who are all running around dating and marrying each other. They are not the majority, but they exist.*

He decided, I believe, to go with the minority on this. And I hope you will too.

Develop an Antenna for Real Life Examples

You can increase your confidence in the reality of wonderful relationships by developing great-relationship radar. A certain percentage of people out there are living exemplars that the HJW kinds are not only a possibility, but a realistic possibility. Start noticing all relationships – young, old, close friends, distant acquaintances, complete strangers. If you persist in expanding your awareness, you will find examples of rewarding, healthy connections. When you see one, acknowledge to yourself that these exist, that some people are having them, and that you will have this soon too. If you get good at this, you won't have to feel as conflicted as Greg did about the future.

To be successful at collecting real life examples though, you must take for granted that these exist. If you do not believe that HJWs exist, you will not be able to perceive them. Here is a real one for you to start with.

Mark is one of the people experiencing a healthy, joyful, whole relationship. He waited until his 30s to get married, despite heavy peer pressure to settle for less than ideal. He was extremely conscious though. He knew himself. He knew that healthy and whole marriages exist. He knew that he wanted one. And, of course, he found one – as most people do tend to land where they set off for. He wants us to understand that anyone who wants HJW partnerships can have them:

Extraordinary relationships exist. I can tell you from first hand experience that they are wonderful and worth aiming for. In my case, it is my marriage. The balance between independence and support is perfect. Our relationship takes very little effort and is a constant source of joy and growth.

I started out, while I was dating, going from one train wreck to the next. They were the types of drama-filled relationships that great movies are made of. Then it occurred to me that it was statistically improbable that all the women in the world were psycho. I eventually concluded that I was the common denominator in all of these fiascos.

I realized that I had no idea what I was really looking for in a relationship. That had to change. I made an exacting list of the attributes I wanted and my list started like this:

> *I want somebody who knows who she is and is not afraid to be herself.*
> *I want somebody who accepts me for who I am.*
> *I want somebody who is honest.*
> *I want somebody who loves.*

After composing this list, I asked myself, who would a person like this be attracted to? The answer seemed to be that the kind of person that matched my points would be drawn to somebody that possessed these same characteristics. Since the first two were not negotiable, I started to work on myself in these key areas. Gradually I noticed that my relationships were getting better and better.

I got a lot of opposition from friends and acquaintances. Numerous people told me that my expectations for marriage were unrealistic. They suggested that I should lower my standards so that I could get married and be happy. At some point, I remember getting angry. In fact, once I said aloud, "I will die single if I have to, but I will not settle."

A few years ago, I met my dream partner. She and I often reflect on how marvelous our relationship is. Of course, we also agree that although our relationship is Heaven on Earth to us, it could be perceived as Hell on Earth to others. We just are perfectly suited to each other.

The Healthy, Joyful, Whole People Are All Running Around with Each Other

You are thinking: *Well, that is very nice that Margaret Ruth knows of the ONE person on the planet having a perfect relationship.* But look closer; Mark's story reveals vital information for all of us. By deciding he was 100% responsible for what was going on, by setting objectives for only truly rewarding connections and by choosing to become more healthy and whole, he found that he was only willing to marry another HJW person. And he is not the only one; there are many more like Mark in the world.

If I had to pick just one truth about relationships I wish was universally understood, it would be this: *All the Healthy, Joyful, Whole People are Running Around – Dating, Mating and Relating – with Each Other*

Similar to the old adage, "Birds of a feather flock together," we all tend to associate socially with people who are roughly like us in terms of emotional, mental and spiritual outlook. It is easier to be close to someone whose *vibe* is in harmony with our own; we think of this as having a rapport or being on each other's wavelength. When HJW people have free choice, they will generally establish more intimate associations with those who are close matches in terms of overall well-being.

It is not that HJW ignore dislike or distain individuals who aren't quite there yet. Many have buddies and friends who wouldn't be generally considered HJW. Even if I was not as healthy and stable as you, we could still enjoy each other's company. We could still bond over our shared love for basketball, beer, and Benicio Del Toro.

What is true is that the closer two people are to each other on an overall scale of well-being, the easier it is to develop close, rewarding bonds. It is under these circumstances that the Law of EEE operates most easily. The smaller a shared overall life outlook is, the harder it is to understand each other. If I only resonate with you on a couple of points, our chances of having an extremely satisfying and rewarding personal connection, a superconscious connection, is low.

Your Job Is to Get on the Healthy Joyful Whole Playground

> Hi Margaret Ruth! I wish more people could get the message about living on the "happy, whole, joyful" playground. We just went to see a friend who called off his wedding; there were just all kinds of bad signs. I kept wanting to tell him, "Dude! You're on the wrong playground!" but I didn't think he'd get it. But you really can't be happy with someone until you're happy with yourself - it really is true! – C.K..

You think, *How do I find these HJW individuals? I hardly know anyone like that.* It is true that the HJW folks are clearly a minority group, comprising maybe 10% of the population. *If that, Margaret Ruth!* - you groan inwardly.

Until we ourselves are fully HJW people, locating the place where all these legendary people might be roaming seems practically impossible. But it is not.

All you have to do is be very healthy, joyful and whole, and you are there.

The good news is that that is all you have to do. Perhaps not an easy thing to do, but it is very simple. This is one of the reasons why we mystics are always talking about You. So much of what you read in the self growth and personal improvement fields focuses on getting you more emotionally, mentally and spiritually healthy, developing a more whole and authentic self, and becoming more happy and joyful. If you are a HJW person, you are automatically operating on the HJW playground because your choices in how you spend your time, and with whom, will be a function of that state.

If you are making those sorts of decisions, you will run around with the other joyful, whole playground playmates who are making the same kinds of choices.

If you know that you are not a perfectly healthy, whole person yet, there is no use in complaining or worrying about your dating or mating life. You will not get a whole, joyful situation till you have done your part and put yourself in a personal place where that outcome is possible. We New Age types are always saying goofy things like "Change yourself - Change your future!" And now you know one reason why.

Where are You Playing Then?

> According to Ellis, healthy people are usually glad to be alive and accept themselves ...They refuse to measure their intrinsic worth by their extrinsic accomplishments, materialistic possessions and by what others think of them. They frankly choose to accept themselves unconditionally; and then try to completely avoid globally rating themselves...They attempt to enjoy rather than prove themselves. – Albert Ellis Institute

Over the years, I have developed a sense of where people land, with respect to their overall vibration of well-being, on what I call the Healthy, Joyful, Whole scale. My approximations stem from reading the inner landscapes of thousands of people. It is a taxonomy based upon how a person feels. It has to be a bit loose then, especially since categorizations and labels can be sometimes as harmful as they are helpful. The problem is of course that every person's uniqueness defies description and no general grouping does justice to the intricate nature of the inner psyche.

But, you might want to peruse my impressions of qualities exhibited by the people on the various levels and see where you might fall.

The categories are based upon the frequency of a person being happy, liking his or her self and liking their life.

For instance, if someone wakes up about 95% of time looking forward to their day, happy about what is happening in life and happy about who s/he is, then s/he is on the 90-100% playground. By the way, this is the place where the HJW people are running around living their HJW lives.

Margaret Ruth's *Find Where You Are* General Playground Chart

Over 90%
Happy, Liking Self, and Liking Life about 90%+ of the time.
Other people and events can be difficult but you deal with them in healthy ways. You have a clear, deep, encompassing self awareness and maintain good boundaries. You anticipate even better things continuing to come into your life. You like all of You, even the goofy parts.

80-90%
Happy, Liking Self, and Liking Life about 80-90% of the time.
You still have some amounts of insecurity, self-criticism and self doubt. You hope your life will bring good things but do not quite trust that it will – almost though. Other people and events can sometimes upset you. You like most of you, most of the time, but sometimes not at all.

70-80%
Happy, Liking Self, and Liking Life about 70-80% of the time.
There are still places inside that are hurt and angry, but you are starting to become aware of this and to understand yourself. You have committed to feeling better, even though it may be unclear how to do this. Other people and events can really shake you up. Other people's opinions of you are pretty important. Sometimes you really doubt your worth.

60-70%

Might be where life can usually seem difficult and draining.

Energy and happiness are sporadic. You are pretty sure you are an ok person but often feel like good things do not happen to you. What people think about you and say to you have the power to change your mood. Shaky sense of self worth makes you require others to notice you and/or approve of you.

Under 60% might be where life seems constantly difficult.

You are constantly drained or ill or anxious or upset. There is very low satisfaction with your life and with others and there might be a general feeling of confusion or emptiness. You may have serious compulsions, obsessions, angers, addictions, health problems or other issues that seriously get in your way of having a happy life.

Less than 65%

This book will not be helpful for anyone who is less than 65% on my rough scale.

If you are in that place, consider getting more grounded and healthy by making appointments with good professional resources such as healers and counselors before making relationships a first priority.

It Takes Two Healthy Joyful Whole People to Make One Healthy Joyful Whole Relationship

Pulling together everything covered so far, you will now realize why this statement is true: *It Takes Two Healthy Joyful Whole People to Make One Healthy Joyful Whole Relationship*. There are no exceptions to this, ever. Another way to put this is that the least healthy person in a relationship will dictate the overall health of the relationship.

Try to imagine two very emotionally unhealthy people enjoying an emotionally healthy relationship. It is hard, no? It turns out that that instead of one half-person plus another half-person making one whole wonderful relationship, the actual math is multiplicative. In intimate relationships especially, what happens is that one half is multiplied by one half and the result is one fourth. Everybody involved is feeling worse by the time it is done.

Instead of feeling expanded by the connection, individuals feel reduced by getting their insecurities and fears magnified in close relationships. This negative personal baggage is what eventually gets multiplied. You have read enough so far to know that this result is Bad.

When two not-emotionally-whole people come together, whatever personal holes exist gets magnified in intimate relationships. What results are intensified **holes,** not **wholes** (Sorry. Could Not Resist that one*).*

But if two Happy, Joyful, Whole people are connecting, it is going to be a Happy, Joyful, Whole interaction.

ISSUE BOX

Objection Margaret Ruth!
I know a very great guy dating a very messed up person. So this is a counterexample to what you say. And you said a counterexample indicates that something is not always true!

This fellow may be great (and I believe that) but he might not be a perfectly healthy person, given what you describe.

Often what we see is that the most healthy person becomes a caretaker to the lesser one. Psychotherapists will explain that being the ongoing unpaid healer/ counselor/parent in an adult entanglement constitutes *not* attending to healthy personal welfare (see the previous chapters). If he is doing that, he has some issues of his own requiring attention.

If he isn't the acting caretaker of the relationship, then he will not date that other person very seriously or for very long. It would be impossible to have an even energy exchange, big girl/big boy, and wholly satisfying, involvement otherwise. And HJW people do not desire to be in anything less than that for their voluntary, close, personal ties.

Wonderful People Connections and What to Have, Do and Be

You set your direction by knowing what you want to have. Knowing what you want implies what you then need to do. Knowing what you want to have and do then leads to knowing what you want to be.

You want to have healthy, joyful, whole relationship experiences. Because of that, what you want to do is hang out on the HJW playground. And then, both objectives require one important thing of you and that is to be the most healthy, joyful, whole You possible.

Simple? Yes. Easy? Maybe not so much. However, close relationships are also your most potent feedback system for informing you of where you are on the HJW scale – if you know how to correctly interpret the feedback.

So if you are not quite where you want to be right now, establishing or developing authentic connections with others will readily help you get there. And you will be happy to know that if you are looking to form those kinds of alliances, there are only Three Things necessary.

Key Points Summary

Whereas Margaret Ruth insists that you have to decide what kinds of relationships you want before we can go any further, therefore implying that she will take her toys and go home if you do not cooperate.

Whereas Margaret Ruth cajoles you to take aim at what you want, begin heading in that direction, and never look back.

Whereas Margaret Ruth decides graciously on everybody's behalf that we want healthy, joyful and whole relationships.

Whereas Margaret Ruth discusses ways that you can get over one typical hurdle and become certain that HJW relationships exist.

Whereas Margaret Ruth presents the shocking news that All the Healthy, Joyful Whole People are All Running Around with Each Other.

Whereas Margaret Ruth declares that she thinks that you should be playing on the Healthy, Joyful, Whole playground.

Whereas Margaret Ruth explains her nifty *Find Where You Are* chart that everyone enjoys so much.

Whereas Margaret Ruth gets all math-y, plays with fractions, and finds it Takes Two Healthy Joyful Whole People to Make One Healthy Joyful Whole Relationship, and that there are no exceptions to this rule although people constantly act as if theirs will be the first exception in history when in reality, seriously, there are no exceptions.

Whereas Margaret Ruth deduces scientifically that because what you want are HJW relationships, what you need to do is get on the HJW playground, and that both of these require you to BE a healthy, joyful, whole You.

Whereas Margaret Ruth runs speedily off towards the next chapter so you can get going on that.

Some Good Further Reads

The Carl Rogers Reader edited by Kirschenbaum and Henderson

A Guide to Rational Living by Albert Ellis with Robert A. Harp

Chapter 5

Only Three Things

Be who you are and say what you feel, because those who mind don't matter and those who matter don't mind. – Dr. Seuss

Deborah's story: When I was a kid, our neighbor Mrs. Pace was perfect. Everyone should be just like her; everyone always said so. My parents said we should try to grow up like Mrs. Pace. Mrs. Pace was always thinking of others. Always sweet and nice. Always pleasant, polite and, of course, perfectly dressed. When I was in my twenties, Mrs. Pace was rushed to the hospital for attempted suicide. So, you see, that was our role model.

The meaningful, satisfying relationships that we've been talking about are not the same as competitive sports, personality contests or profit ventures. There is no competition for who gets what, who likes whom and who doesn't, no head fakes, no bait and switch, no sucker punches and no prize – no prestige, no popularity, no posse and certainly no free cabana boys (you will have to hire them) – other than very rewarding interpersonal experiences.

And developing these real and rewarding relationships, the kind the young radio caller in Chapter 1 was aching for, will require only Three Things.

You and the Symphony You Play

It is breathtakingly simple. Envision that you are a composer and recording artist, of a sort, whose job it is to broadcast what is going on with You. The various sections of your inner self produce the melodies and tunes that will play. Picture the all the parts of you as the instruments of this inner orchestra – or full-on funk band if you like – in there.

If the sound produced is to be vibrant, compelling and original you will take care to listen to all the notes, rhythms and cadences and then fine-tune and adjust as you see best for your composition. Once you find a true and clear sound, you offer it to others. They might applaud. They might boo and throw tomatoes. That is completely their decision to make. What others think about your vibrational composition is not your job; it's theirs.

The feedback can be beneficial though. Maybe a positive reaction or critical comment seems helpful and you decide to use it to improve and harmonize your personal work of art. Further, if someone takes sincere interest in your broadcast and responds, an opening for a connection with another is created.

If you reciprocate, you complete a meaningful interpersonal exchange.

Only Three Things

There are only Three Things you need to do for your half of voluntary, personal and adult relationships. You must understand your own truth; your expression must reflect what is true for you; you must fully realize that others' reactions to your truth are not your responsibility.

There are only Three Things and no more:

1 **Know your truth**
2 **Express your truth**
3 ~~**Reactions to your truth**~~ **[Blank – others' reactions are not your job]**

Doing the Three Things is very much like know your self, be your self and let others be their selves. If you are sure of what is true for you, then you will be able to fully express that. If you express who you really are and what is really going on for you, then you give someone a chance to get to know and maybe even understand you. If someone is interested in what you are expressing, there is now an opening for a meaningful connection.

And there is more to consider. If you do not offer an authentic you, then to whom are we supposed to relate? Some representation that is only sort-of-you? A pale representation of you? A person that is hardly even you? As you can tell from my rhetorical questions, if you try to alter or conceal what is true, then your personal connections will be weak. If the other person is not relating to the real you, it will be hard to feel fulfilled by that kind of relationship.

Don't get confused over impersonal, professional and distant associations by thinking these are the same as personal bonds; cultivate discernment of what kind of involvement you are dealing with.

The Three Things do not apply to impersonal, distant or non-voluntary relationships such as with a boss, a police officer, an acquaintance or the person sitting next to us on the plane.

We are not required to conduct a social, meaningful interaction with everyone.

There are few reasons to spill out all our authenticity to the parking meter lady, the manager, the neighbor guy or the judge.

If you know your whole self, and express it as clearly as you can, then how we react to it is out of your control and is not even your job. That's our job. This is a certainty because of the 100-0 Law.

Our relationship framework looks like this now:

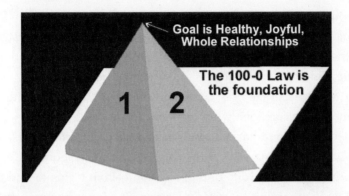

Thing 1: Know What Is True for You

> Shrek: NO! LAYERS! Onions have layers. OGRES have layers. Onions have layers... you get it. We both have layers. – *Shrek* (film)

Thing 1 is that you must know yourself and what is true for you. I think that most of us intellectually understand that it is hard for others to have a real connection to us if we are not being our real self. A mutual bond can be no truer than the people involved.

If you believe ideal relationships are the ones wherein you get to be yourself and be appreciated for exactly who you are now, you have no choice but to find out what *being yourself* and *who you are* means. If you and I don't do this for ourselves, then we leave an opening for others to define us.

If you are fully self-aware then you will broadcast a very clear signal, which will be easier to pick up and easier to understand by the others. If you have ever dealt with someone who said one thing, did another altogether and appeared not to mean any of it, you will recognize the confusion inherent in attempting to connect with someone with a mixed broadcast.

The shorthand for Thing 1 is to *know your truth*. It is not perfectly apt because the phrase implies there is just one truth for you. Now that is hard to find. A key point about trying to find the real you is that you are a complex person. Honor being multidimensional and take on this job of comprehending it all. Develop an enduring sense of the entirety of the You that is relating to the others and a perfect inner radar that constantly scans and advises.

A Psychic Aside: You Are Always Broadcasting

You might as well be truthful because at some level you are usually broadcasting practically everything anyway and anyone tuned in well enough will pick it up.

The information we throw off is discernable through physical expressions like body language, mental expressions like words and sentences and energetic composition, which is the tricky one because we cannot measure or objectively quantify that part of our total selves.

You can envision this as *vibes, energy or aura* – as we discussed when picturing the *Prime You* in Chapter 2. You might have heard phrases like: *Her vibe was positive; I couldn't be around that guy's energy.*

Know that every single dimension, each part, of you contributes to the information that you throw off. I know I can, as can many others, read a person who is not physically present and whom I have never met. I use inner senses to locate a particular person and will usually get an energetic understanding of what is going on with them.

The fact that this can be done with a high amount of accuracy (and I want you to know everyone can do this if they want) means that humans are more than physical and have more than just five senses to use for gathering information. Sometimes these extra antennas are called the sixth sense, intuition, the quantum field or extra-sensory-perception (ESP). I usually refer to data that cannot be attained by the five senses as psychic or metaphysical information.

Of course, there are always those who insist these hokum psychic hookups **cannot** be done and anyone with a brain knows there are **only** five senses! To which I say, *Hey - good luck with that*, and turn my valuable attention back to actual reality where in fact many, many people have personally experienced metaphysical information – a premonition, a flash, an energy, a vision or a knowing – for themselves.

Thing 2: Express What Is True for You

I am trying to play the truth of what I am. It is difficult because I'm changing all the time. – Charles Mingus

The second Thing is to express yourself genuinely, meaning that if you choose to communicate, it must be true for you. What you do and how you act needs to be authentic and if you decide to open your mouth, what falls out it must an honest expression.

It is understandable to not always fully express ourselves in impersonal and non-personal situations. But, it seems obvious that if the goal is extremely satisfying connections with others, you cannot avoid the requirement that when choosing to communicate, you do it in a way that is true for you. When you do this, people will know who you really are and they will be able to trust you.

If someone continually indicates sentiments that are not true or only partially true, s/he will have problems developing strong interpersonal bonds. A good example is an old friend of mine, Paige, who in the name of being "nice" always said, "Yes, I can go," even when she did not really want to or could not really make it because of other commitments (that she had also said "Yes" to). Paige created all of the following results at one time or another from this truth-avoidance-in-order-to-be-nice behavior:

She
    Had no fun
    Ended up canceling anyway
    Spent the entire time fidgeting
    Was late
The friends were exposed to her
    Lack of enthusiasm
    Lack of commitment
    Lack of punctuality

And yet, Paige's other friends rarely called her on this, because they were also trying to be "nice," thus perpetuating the problems. Although I really liked Paige, it eventually became more difficult to include her than not, as I never really knew if she would be there, on time and, if she came, if she really wanted to be there.

If some people habitually don't understand and acknowledge the truth about themselves – their opinions, their preferences, or their feelings – then they will create some or many of the following results:

Discomfort in his/her own skin
Empty feelings
Numbness
Not knowing who she really is
Not knowing how he really feels
Lack of trust in his or herself
Needing others to fill in those blanks

This last is a serious problem because the person who cannot tell what's personally true has also created a situation where:

People do not know him
People do not understand her
People do not believe him
People do not trust her

Relating your truth is simpler and healthier for you. One terrific benefit of being authentic is that you become less available to people trying to get you to change what you say. If you express something that is true for you – for instance: *I'm tired* – and others want you to change, alter or ignore it, you won't be able to change your tiredness to suit them no matter how hard pressed.

Amidst the Droppings and Trappings – Be Clear

When applying for jobs, most of us have to fill out an application or present a resume. It is necessary. Just like resume presentations, name-dropping, credential-dropping and association-trappings are forms of personal expression too. Displaying these identifications is usually designed to influence others to think a particular way about us – usually to think more highly. Seeking to increase credibility, status or desirability, we sometimes use our associations and credentials to enhance our image. This could also apply to possessions, clothes, cars and trips.

If you and I decide to display our feathers, it is not necessarily a bad thing. If we need to persuade others by presenting a resume, status enhancements or vestiges of prestigious associations, it can be for very good reasons, such as trying to get a job. But it is best to be clear about the *what* and the *why* of it because doing so gives others an opening to identify us with these droppings and trappings. We risk also giving them permission to influence the sense of self worth if these become more important than the real person.

But if you decide to do this, and are clear about what you are doing and do not give the trappings and droppings the power to define you, there's no problem. The man (or woman) makes the clothes, not the other way around. Just be clear.

Thing 3: Others' Reactions to Your Truth

Those who are meant to hear will understand. Those who are not meant to understand will not hear. – Confucius

Thing 3 is other people's reactions to what you decide to express. Thing 3 is essentially a Black Mystery Hole that is not anywhere near your orbit of control, nor is it your responsibility, nor truly any of your business.

Because of the 100-0 Law, Thing 1 and Thing 2 are 100% your business. On the other hand, what others choose as a response is 0% your job. Like shooting a basketball, once you have communicated your authentic expression and that ball leaves your metaphorical hands, how others perceive and receive it is now out of your influence.

It is not your job in a relationship to react to your expressions or be in charge of what other people think – it is their job. Plus, you cannot even control what others think of your truth so if you make it your business to do this, then you will be perpetually stressed. Without their permission, you cannot even influence their choices of in how they react to you.

People confused about who is responsible for Thing 3 find relationships to be quite stressful and certainly are often guilty of claiming that *Relationships take (arduous back-breaking) work you know!*

Authentic Two-Way Connections

It was impossible to get a conversation going, everybody was talking too much. – Yogi Berra

When another sets his tuner on your broadcast, an open link starts.

The simple psychic truth is that a possible connection opens when someone literally and figuratively tunes into your wavelength, or matches your vibe, or turns their attention dial to the channel where you are broadcasting.

Does that way of thinking about connecting sound strange to you? If so, you can safely skip that last paragraph because your personal everyday observations and experience will also reveal that connections start when two people pay attention to each other. Even the phrase, *pay attention,* indicates that somebody is expending energy and focusing upon something. You already know that you feel very nice when another indicates understanding or interest in the real you.

Most of us have experienced a time when our eyes met with a stranger's and there was a moment of understanding, or connection, before we turned away and back to whatever or whoever was commanding our main attention. Can you remember this? It is hard to find words to describe what it was that got exchanged for that brief second. But the *exchange* is what identifies it as a complete connection.

It sounds simple, and it is, but there is always some confusion about what is or is not a possible connection. Try this visualization. Picture yourself at a party where you do not know the other guests and are trying to start a conversation. *I like Dogs*, you state. This is good if you really do like dogs without any conflicting ideas about it (whereupon the true statement would be: *I have conflicting thoughts about dogs*).

Here are various responses you might get:

1. I do too!
2. Let me tell you some of my funny jokes about dogs so the focus can be on me because I'm such a comedian.
3. What a weird idea.
4. What kind of dog do you have?
5. I don't just like dogs, I love dogs. I am like that. I am a wonderful person in so many ways. Let me count them for you while we are on that topic.
6. Where's the bar?

My view is that 1 and 4 tuned in and attended enough to your honest expression to indicate an open connection. If you reciprocate, you complete the circuit. Also check what you perceived about the responses. Do you agree that 1 and 4 tuned in? Can you see why I don't think the others were connecting?

Sticking to your truth allows better discrimination between potentially rewarding links and those that aren't. If you state something truthful and someone wants to, gloss over it, belittle you, tell you that you don't know what you are talking about, tries to change your truth, doesn't accept it, won't hear it, or anything similar, then why would you want to develop closer ties a person like that? Keep that one at arm's length.

If someone consistently cannot hear your truth, and you double check to make sure you did the first and second Things as well as you could, then you must seriously reconsider why you are attempting to have a close relationship with that person.

After you speak what is true for you and someone hears it and either understands it or wants to hear more, an authentic connection has started. If you hear and comprehend the other's genuine truth, that connection is completed. This bond can be considered authentic and real because it develops between two people appreciating each other while being perfectly themselves.

If the connection is to get repeated enough to become a relationship, where there is a mutual desire to keep the exchanges going, there has to be some sort of mental, psychic, physical or emotional reward for both people and some sort of way to keep the exchange going through visits, calls, letters or emails. The relationship bond gets built up from finding these ongoing opportunities for sharing ideas, emotions, touches, information and experiences. If these exchanges are valued and fairly even, and so are mutually rewarding, people will want to continue them.

Two Way Connections

To connect to the internet, my laptop has a radar screen showing me the various wireless networks in the vicinity. I have to click on a wireless provider icon and, if everything lines up ok, there is a connection. The system and my computer recognize each other and a path to trade information forms. Nothing will happen though without me forming an intent to notice or look at something.

Also, it seems to me that if the wireless provider

nodule-thingy wasn't really sure what it should be, or wonders what I want it to be in order for me to like it, and kept changing forms and identities so to be popular and well liked, then I would struggle to find it. I'm just saying

People connections are similar. There are many, many people out there and our personal radar picks up a bunch of that broadcasting from around us. Our attention goes to some of that (and where it goes depends upon our individual and unique inner landscape).

When we focus our attention on something, we are directing some part of our energy towards it: our time, thoughts, emotions and the act of physical observation. If we seek to understand, identify or interact with it, we can begin a connection. If whatever it is gives us some energy, attention or information back then the connection now goes both ways.

Testing, Testing, 1-2-3, Testing...

This morning I saw someone's comment to a blog article of mine and my first reaction was a bad-feeling-anger-zing that went something like this: *What is that guy's problem? He seems to have either not read the whole piece or missed the whole point! How dare he criticize!*

I wish I could relate that this reaction only lasted a millisecond but it honestly bothered me for several minutes – until I consciously noticed my feelings about it. Dealing with the unpleasant feelings took me that long, even after understanding how to do the Three Things for all these years.

There is a signal indicating that you might not be doing one or more of the Three Things completely and it is noticing, during an exchange or when thinking about it later, you get a negative reaction or feeling. This negative sensation needs to be associated with the interaction and not with understandable stimuli like a stomach ache or someone yelling at you. But, if you get an unpleasant reaction like mine from an interaction, and then stop to take a moment to reflect on where you might have not fully accomplished the Three Things, you have a chance to further develop self awareness.

Sometimes you can tell what you are doing wrong, such as having trouble being honest. Sometimes it is not obvious and requires much more investigation.

I ask myself questions such as: *Did I feel attached to or responsible for the other's reaction? Was my communicating clear and meaningful? Did I acknowledge what was really true for me? Or did I gloss over something really true in the name of brevity, or convenience, or to be nice, and now it's bugging me?*

Doing that this morning, I found two incomplete Things that caused the negative pop in me. The first was that I was not entirely letting this other person own his reaction. By taking it as a slam, even for a second, against my intellect and writing ability, I was still holding an assumption that I could influence this other's thinking with my wildly extravagant talent I guess, and so I was violating Thing 3.

After I got past that little business, I wondered if maybe the article wasn't perfectly clear thus causing his confusion. Therefore, I decided that Thing 2 also needed attention in this case and reviewed the article one more time for clarity.

However, discovering and mending our stuff is usually not as easy as my simple case. Most of the time, deeper exploration is needed.

Your homework assignment is to boldly participate in as many interactions as possible while paying minute attention to your decisions, actions and feelings in order to get a sense of how well you do each of the Three Things.

If there is an area that needs more explanation and practice, the next chapters will cover these specific topics in depth for you: *knowing what it true for you, expressing your truth, assigning others absolute responsibility for their reactions, understanding how satisfying relationships form, using relationship reactions as potent openings for personal expansion.*

Key Points Summary

There are only Three Things necessary for meaningful, real connections:

1. Know what is true for you
2. Express yourself truthfully
3. BLANK (Other people's reactions to your truth are not your job)

Thing 1 can be difficult because it requires you to be fully aware of each part of you inner symphony and know what is true for all of you.

Thing 2 requires authentic self expression so that you don't broadcast mixed signals. You want people to know the real you and to trust you.

Thing 3 is impossible to do because of the 100-0 Law and so others' choice of reaction is 100% their responsibility.

If you speak what is true for you and someone shows interest by tuning in, an authentic connection begins. If you pay attention to the other's genuine truth in turn, that connection is completed.

If you are certain of what is true for you and express it, and someone continually cannot hear or accept your truth, you must sincerely ask yourself if you should attempt having a very close bond with that person (answer = no).

Noticing when an unpleasant or bad feeling associated with your interactions helps to spot when you are not doing the Three Things completely. Reading the forthcoming specific chapter for each will help fix that and you will feel better about your involvements very soon.

Further Good Reads

Conversations with God: An Uncommon Dialogue by Neale Donald Walsch

The Four Agreements by Don Miquel Ruiz

Chapter 6

Thing 1: Tune In, Tune Up

We have all a better guide in ourselves, if we would attend to it, than any
other person can be. – Jane Austen

*Abby came to see me today. She hated her reading. After years of no
dates or romance, she had almost convinced herself that marriage would
never happen for her, she said. She desperately wanted to know when,
how, who and where she would "meet someone." When I told her that
she would be having smaller flirtations in the near future, which would
evolve into more serious medium-sized relationships, followed by finally
meeting someone to fall in love with, she fell apart emotionally over the
length of time involved.*

*I explained that when I was reading her, I found a mixed bag of
beliefs, fears and desires, and as long as it was like this, she would get
mixed results. She heartily disagreed, "No, I am sure that I am ready
now. I don't think I have mixed feelings at all. In fact, if this fellow in
Denver isn't going to 'work out' why bother going on the trip at all?"
Her face turned red and teary.*

*Abby wasn't looking deep enough. Her inner sensor wouldn't go
past the surface. Part of her retained negative beliefs and feelings from
past hurts, all the while her insecurities were feeding desperation. She
had a probable future where she's dating someone in a more serious
manner and it does not "work out." While in reality those future mixed
results simply reflect her own mixed psyche, the episode will seem to
just validate her fears and doubts. She will be physically, mentally and
emotionally wounded again and, again, not understand why. I asked
Abby: "Don't you want to avoid that?"*

*I don't know if she understood what I told her about those confused
and damaging parts of herself. I doubt she'll be back.*

Completely finding our truth is not something many of us are good at. However, doing Thing 1 requires that you know what is true for you, and so it begins with deeply exploring your personal complexities. From there, you can start retraining the parts of the inner orchestra that are singing a lousy song or, in other words, telling you things that are not true.

This is tricky because many people believe that who they are consists of what they are *thinking* at the moment. But, humans are not just their thoughts. Most of us are a jumble of internal dialog, feelings, ideas, beliefs, instincts, expectations, attitudes, memories and desires.

Have you ever had a relationship where the other person was erratic or constantly giving off mixed messages? This is because the person was mixed up, had mixed feelings, and was thus broadcasting mixed vibrations.

You could say that his or her symphony was not in harmony. And the wild thing is that a certain percentage of those discordant folks will INSIST that *No, I am perfectly consistent and coherent. What is your problem??*

You Have Layers

Some compare it to peeling an onion. In awareness, we observe without evaluation or judgment each layer and move on to the next. Beneath all the layers of the false self's automatic beliefs, judgments, negative emotions and striving, we find the Self. – Tony D'Souza and Bud Wonsiewicz

Becoming aware of the many layers of your psyche that are continually chattering on (OR SOMETIMES SHOUTING REALLY LOUDLY SO AS TO DROWN THE OTHER PARTS OUT) will help you understand the whole of you. I can hear them when I'm doing a reading and you can hear your various inner selves too, if you practice.

I drew up a picture of the multiple messages, ideas, feelings and reactions that go on inside a person. It is an amalgam of what goes on in inside many of us; some of which is chattering away right now beneath your own surface awareness.

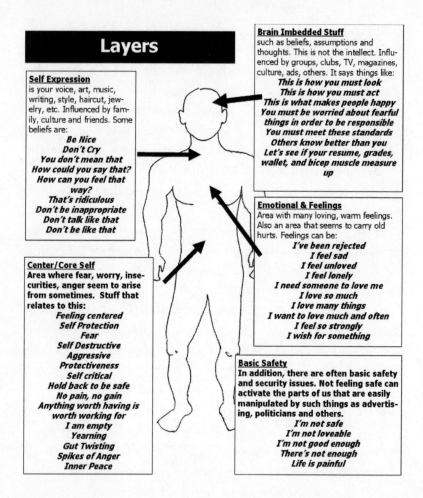

Layers

Self Expression
is your voice, art, music, writing, style, haircut, jewelry, etc. Influenced by family, culture and friends. Some beliefs are:
Be Nice
Don't Cry
You don't mean that
How could you say that?
How can you feel that way?
That's ridiculous
Don't be inappropriate
Don't talk like that
Don't be like that

Brain Imbedded Stuff
such as beliefs, assumptions and thoughts. This is not the intellect. Influenced by groups, clubs, TV, magazines, culture, ads, others. It says things like:
This is how you must look
This is how you must act
This is what makes people happy
You must be worried about fearful things in order to be responsible
You must meet these standards
Others know better than you
Let's see if your resume, grades, wallet, and bicep muscle measure up

Emotional & Feelings
Area with many loving, warm feelings. Also an area that seems to carry old hurts. Feelings can be:
I've been rejected
I feel sad
I feel unloved
I feel lonely
I need someone to love me
I love so much
I love many things
I want to love much and often
I feel so strongly
I wish for something

Center/Core Self
Area where fear, worry, insecurities, anger seem to arise from sometimes. Stuff that relates to this:
Feeling centered
Self Protection
Fear
Self Destructive
Aggressive
Protectiveness
Self critical
Hold back to be safe
No pain, no gain
Anything worth having is worth working for
I am empty
Yearning
Gut Twisting
Spikes of Anger
Inner Peace

Basic Safety
In addition, there are often basic safety and security issues. Not feeling safe can activate the parts of us that are easily manipulated by such things as advertising, politicians and others.
I'm not safe
I'm not loveable
I'm not good enough
There's not enough
Life is painful

Sit back for a moment, do an inner scan and see if you can find any internal dialog going on right now. How many of these are going on inside you? Many? Few? None? Oddly enough, often times when we turn our focus inward, it all gets kind of quiet in there. However, I have an effective exercise that helps you get to know all of the various parts of your inner orchestra and hear what tunes they are playing.

Exercise: Tune In – Listening to Your Symphony

It has to be able to play at the maximum expression and communication in every style, and the only way you can do that is - like Verdi said - working with a file, every day, little by little, until the orchestra's collective qualities emerge. – James Levine

If your inner symphony isn't perfectly harmonious, which would make you like most of us, a good first step is to get a sense of exactly what tunes are being played in there. Knowing exactly, on every level, what is going on with you might also be termed perfect self awareness, which is required in order to become fully healthy, joyful and whole, and is described by additional phrases such as self knowledge, self actualization and self discovery.

Here is an effective exercise that helps you more fully understand the ongoing stream of the many parts of you. Try *Listening to Your Symphony* as many times as you can, as long as it seems helpful. Learning what the different parts of you are saying and sound like can help you understand at any given time what part seems to be directing your inner landscape. It also helps you realize how much is really going on with you.

Set up

Pick a time when there seems to be a jumble of ideas, feelings and thoughts going on. This exercise is especially effective when you are feeling very confused, upset, angry or afraid as these are the times when more inner parts of you are active.

You will need to write the results down. Some people use paper and pencil/pen and some use a blank word processing page. You will need a hefty sized alone time, especially at first. Also, be in a place where interruptions are minimal. Back porches, private bathrooms and walk in closets are all good.

The steps

Open a blank page and get ready to write down what comes up.

Your job is to picture yourself as a psychologist or journalist. So close your eyes, focus on the inner self and tell your jumble of thoughts and voices that you are going to examine each one of them, one at a time. Assure your inner self you will be recording everything each part of you wants to say without interference, editing or arguing.

Ask now: *Who is first?*

Using your inner senses, listen to the first voice or stream of thought that comes through. Start writing down everything it is saying.

The first voice that comes through is often a very loud, fearful, critical and mean sort of voice, especially if you pick a confused, upsetting time to do all this. For the first few paragraphs, you might find yourself agreeing or disagreeing or wanting to edit what you are hearing. Don't do that. Just keep saying, *ok, ok, what next?* It might pause. You always say to it: *Anything else? What next?* Keep going until it is completely done.

It can often take pages to get through the first voice's litany of criticisms, fears and angers. Keep saying: *Ok, ok, what next?* This loud critical one will finally come down to something like, *Your car is dirty and your socks don't match.*

You ask, *Anything else?* You get nothing. And so, that is one down.

Now, focus inward and say: *Who is Next?*

This second voice is often quite difficult. Our most vulnerable self (think Your Inner Child) is usually right underneath the mean loud one and so is often the next one you hear. It can be excruciatingly emotional to listen to this one, so people sometimes block this part of themselves. However, do not do this.

The usual second voice has the power to make us break down because it is so frightened, lonely and raw. You are not allowed to interfere in this particular exercise with any of your inner voices, EXCEPT THIS ONE. You might have to talk directly to it when it tells you how afraid it is for its happiness and safety. Picture this extremely tender part of you as a kitten or baby bird. Visualize taking it out of yourself, wrapping it in a blanket and cuddling it on your shoulder. Tell it that you will not let it get hurt.

But, as you continually reassure your vulnerable self, keep asking it *What else?* and write what you get. Eventually it will be done and the good news is that this voice doesn't talk nearly as long as the first loud mean one.

After these tougher parts are done, it is an easy road to the finish now. The next group of voices is usually more medium in volume and emotional heft.

Ask again: *Who is next?* Let the next voice come through, *What does it want to say?* Record it all and keep asking *Anything else?* When that one is done, ask, *Who is next?*

These more medium toned voices can be hard to distinguish. If you do not know which part of you is speaking, you can always ask *Who are you?* It will tell you something like "I am the adventure part of you!" or "I am the business part of you and I am telling you that you are wasting your time with all this inner stuff." Sometimes these inner selves will give you a title, or a name, or a picture to indicate what their specific role is in the maintenance and well-being of You.

Keep going and ask *Who is Next? Anything Else?*

Eventually, if you let it, you will get to parts of you that might seem to have softer and lighter tones. You might start feeling buzzy, tingly or energized. Ask them who they are. These parts of you could be your higher self, your inner guidance and, if you keep going, you could come to a part of you that says something like "We are your guides."

If you get this far, notice how the messages from this part of your orchestra have such a contrasting flavor to the first voices. They will often say things like: "You are doing very well;" "I am enjoying your life experience;" "We know you to be a special spirit." Cool stuff like that.

Now you cannot argue with or edit these guys either. You will want to say, *Oh no, I'm not!* But, again, no interfering – just record it all and say: *Uh-huh, yes, I'm special, yes, anything else?*

Keep going until every one is done

If you allow it, you can come to a point where there will be no response to *Who's next*. At this point, take a moment, bask and completely soak in the feelings, sensations, visuals, sounds, tastes and smells of when the entire orchestra, comprised of all the parts of you, is quiet.

For as long as this silence lasts, try to absorb every bit of it that you can, so that you can readily recall the experience of having all the chatter off. Soak it in until, you know, until the Headline News inner-tickers start up again with "You really should be balancing your checkbook," "I'm hungry," and "Where are my shoes?"

There's More

> Every human being has hundreds of separate people living under his skin. The talent of a writer is his ability to give them their separate names, identities, personalities and have them relate to other characters living with him. – Mel Brooks

Now close your notebook or word processing. Mentally step aside and ponder these questions for some moments. Which part of you was listening and doing all the writing? And, then, what part of you was the space at the end, the space that was so quiet, felt so calm and where you couldn't hear any of the internal dialogs?

Spoiler: The answer is You with a capital Y because it is your core and essential self that you find when all the chatter and other stuff goes away. It is the You that does all the listening to the internal dialog and thought processes.

Go as often as you can to that memory feeling of that last quiet space, especially when confused, upset, down. The more you can recall who You really are, and discriminate between your essential self and the sounds of your fears, desires, ideas and the others, the more self aware you will be.

I assure you that you will really, really, really, like meeting You. The feeling that connection generates is indescribable. It makes it worth going through all those layers and listening to all of that chatter to arrive in that centered, clear space that is the heart of You.

Listen to Your Symphony Recap

- Pick a time when your feelings and/or thoughts seem really jumbled and you also have some time to yourself.
- Start with paper/pen or blank computer word processing page.
- You will allow each one of your inner parts, or voices, speak its peace in its entirety, one at time.
- You will write down what you are hearing from these parts of the symphony without editing or arguing.
- You will say: *Who is next?* And keep asking *Anything else?* until each one is completely finished.
- Keep going until there is no answer to *Who is next?*
- Absorb and remember the sensations when all the inner talk is quiet (this is the reward for your efforts and reveals something important about You)

Stuffing
Stuffing is burying emotions so deeply, that you would usually not know these are there until there is a highly charged emotional situation (like a fight or emergency) OR

---

until you get good at listening to all parts of your symphony.

Stuffing your emotions is not recommended either by psychologists or by psychics as it is bad for you physically, emotionally and energetically. Don't stuff your feelings and if you have already done this – and almost everyone over the age of 12 probably has – make sure you understand what you have buried in there.

The metaphysical truth is the same as what psychologists want you to realize: It will come out sooner or later, in one way or another. Make an appointment with a good psychotherapist if this is a difficult area for you as these folks are trained to help people deal with this and other similar issues.

A Shorter Version: Talk Directly to the Problem Parts

You can use a shorter, more direct version of the symphony exercise to get clear too. This is where you allow a part of you, one that is really upset, to do a data dump.

My friend Chrissy explained in frustration that she always feels like a race horse that is pulling at her bit, wanting to gallop forward a break neck speed. But there is a mean little jockey inside who, not wanting Chrissy to break her neck, is constantly pulling in sharply and holding her back.

Because she is a friend of mine and I know she won't sit still for longer (and yet so wonderful) Margaret Ruth exercises, I gave her a shortened version and you might like this better too.

My sense was that Chrissy would not be able to simply release the protective jockey part of her self, as it was exactly that: protective. But, if she could get it to play a new more cooperative tune, the tension could lighten by generating just a bit more harmony.

Talk to her, I suggested. Have a conversation with the jockey who won't let you go and ask her what her story is. Let her tell you everything she wants. Take notes and let her go on and on until she is done telling you what her problems with you are. Don't argue with her or edit her, at first. Be like a journalist that is just taking notes. Just keep saying to her: *Yes, go on...anything else?*

When she is done with her no-doubt-long list of issues, engage her. What needs to happen for her to let go of the reins? What does she need to know, or you need to do, to make this a more cooperative venture between your desire to get going with your life and her desire to slow you down. See if there is a way you can work together.

She reported some interesting results. Her jockey basically said she did not trust Chrissy as Chrissy had gotten into some very bad situations in the past. Chrissy is not trustworthy when it comes to taking care of Chrissy, according to the jockey.

She had asked, *What would it take for the jockey to let go?* The answer was that the jockey was not going to let go anytime soon but was willing to soften up just a little bit. The jockey proclaimed that Chrissy would need to prove she was being mindful and taking better care of herself. If that happens, the jockey would let go a little bit more. By doing this exercise, Chrissy was able to feel less conflicted very quickly; she reported recently that the jockey is only lightly holding her back now.

Her example also shows us also why gaining inner harmony helps you avoid getting mixed results in the actions you take; all your metaphorical inner horses will be headed in the same direction instead of arguing and working against each other.

Re-tuning for What is Really True For You

Feelings are sometimes difficult to discover – and often even more difficult to acknowledge. Yet hidden in your deepest feelings is your highest truth. The trick is to get to those feelings… If you want to know what's true for you about something, look to how you're feeling about it. – Neale Donald Walsch

Old assumptions and beliefs that are not true, such as *I'm not good enough*, are often buried and they will continue to affect your ability to send a clear and authentic signal – and weaken your capacity to feel healthy, joyful, whole. Once you start becoming more aware, it is important to be able to cut through the clutter and sort inner messages and ideas for truth.

The 100% Accurate Test for Finding What is True for You exercise gives you detailed instructions on how to replace inner beliefs that are not true for you with those that are. The process of reformatting embedded inner dialog into personal truth will make an enormous difference in your ability to have the relationships that you want, in addition to simply allowing you to feel better, which is also a great payoff.

I have found that people can get to a point where the process of trying to release old beliefs, negative self talk and unhealthy attitudes gets stalled or stuck; parts of us simply won't go and keep droning the same critical, fearful or insecure messages. The method that works is to re-tune those orchestra sections with different songs to sing, so to speak. The ideal replacement messages are statements that are true. Here is how to do this.

We each have inside of us what other metaphysical authors have termed an inner guidance system, an inner wisdom or the inner knower. Our inner system has a foolproof, perfectly accurate way of letting us know when we are telling ourselves something, somewhere, that isn't true. It is a negative sensation or reaction like a bad feeling, a throat clench, anxiety or a sad emotion.

These negative reactions are your signal that some part of you is muttering something that is not true for you. If there is not an outside stimulus like a fire, upsetting information, someone yelling or an actual moose chasing you – and you are just sitting there experiencing some sort of negative emotion or reaction – then somewhere the system has hit on and is processing an untrue message, thought or belief. You can think of it as hitting on a programming logic error.

It is very important that you understand that the zing, pop, hit or sensation of a negative feeling or reaction is a 100% accurate indicator that somewhere in there, you are chewing on something that isn't true. Without fully accepting that, this exercise will not work. It is too easy to brush negative reactions aside without looking hard and long at the underlying false beliefs and ideas that are causing the negative hit.

You can test whether a thought or statement is true for you – or not – also with a feeling. Things that are true for you sit very quietly, neutrally and softly. For instance, I tell you, "Hey, you're reading right now." Your reaction is probably something like "That's right." It's true and should sit very neutrally on you and not cause any angst or negative feeling at all (*unless there is some sort of guilt about reading right now, in which case the negative sensation says your guilt is a program logic error and something you are telling yourself is not true*).

Exercise: Tune Up – *The 100% Accurate Test for Finding What is True for You*

The exercise has three steps. Notice when you are having an internal negative reaction, find the belief, assumption or idea – obvious or hidden – being processed that is false for you, and rewrite it into a statement that is actually true.

The number one point to remember is that your internal sensor of what is true for you is 100% accurate, 100% of the time.

Any time your inner processing system is chewing on, talking about or bumping into something that isn't true for you, you will get a negative reaction inside there: feelings, gut clenches, teeth grinding, sorrow, and stomach drop. These somethings that aren't true for you can be thoughts, beliefs, ideas, assumptions or conclusions. They can be right on the surface of your thoughts or buried far below those thoughts on top. Wherever it is, it is *not* true for you. If you ignore the signal and do not take the time to pursue the underlying false belief, nothing changes.

The second important point is realizing the key to getting your inner landscape cleared of untrue stuff as quickly as possible is to write down the new, true statements.

You and I can track down inner parts chattering false beliefs and assumptions all we want, but if these are not replaced with the new truth, the same tune will continue to be played, over and over. We won't get the result we want.

Get Started

The *100% Accurate Test for Finding What is True for You* exercise requires having a little notebook or paper with you all the time.

Step 1. Notice whenever you are having a negative reaction

The signal is a zing, pop, hit, sensation of something that does not feel good and is not associated with an appropriate outside stimulus. A bad feeling, gut clench, heart ache and agitation are examples. Stop and notice this going on and say to yourself something like:

> *Somewhere I am telling myself something that isn't true.*
> *Somewhere in the internal processor, the system has hit a logic error and an alarm is going off.*
> My favorite is: *Somewhere in there I am chewing on something that isn't true.*

Step 2. Find what you were telling yourself that isn't true by testing for the feelings a statement generates.

Things that are true for you will sit very neutrally, quietly. Things that are not true will cause a negative feeling or reaction. The hardest part of step 2 is getting to the bottom of it. Be willing to keep peeling the layers until you find the idea that is causing the negative feeling. Here's a fast track hint: most of the time, the bottom line will be buried beliefs of *I am not good enough, I won't be ok, or I am not loveable*.

Important: Once you find what it is that you are chewing upon that is causing the bad reaction, understand that the negative reaction exactly indicates it is not true for you.

Step 3. Replace the idea/thought/belief that isn't true with something that is true by testing for that easy, neutral feeling.

Write down things that might be more true than the thought currently held and test each one. Keep going until you come up with the idea that sits as easily and naturally as you can find. Write that one down and underline it, memorize it, have it handy. This third step is the most important one. It is important that you write down the things that are true - this will quicken and magnify the results.

At first the three steps for re-tuning are quite cumbersome. When you begin trying this, each of the three parts is difficult and time consuming. However, if you keep going, testing for what is true for you can become a habitual response. Just like changing any habit, after three weeks you get pretty good at it. Do it for three months and the process becomes quick and easy. You can eventually get so clever at spotting stuff that isn't true that all it will take is noticing small disruptions like anxiously tapping your foot or crunching ice, and you will be able to get to a calmer place very quickly. And this is a wonderful way to live your life, for the rest of your life.

Finding Your Personal Truth **does not imply a need to act on impulses that are harmful to others.**

It could be *true* for someone that he wants to kick his brother in the shins, but having that desire does not imply that it should be done. Can you see the difference between noticing what is true — with feelings like *I am angry, or I am revengeful* — for the moment, and believing these sorts of thoughts should be acted upon since they are true feelings? They **shouldn't** be acted on just because it is true that those feelings are occurring.

A good rule of thumb is to avoid physically, emotionally, mentally or verbally harming another. One reason, in addition to what I just wrote above, is harming someone doesn't really work to solve the real problem (unless of course it is understandable self defense). The real problem is usually you and your inner conflicts,

> insecurities and fears. Another good reason for this rule is harming others is Bad for you, and for them too.

Two Case Examples

> What is Truth? A difficult question; but I have solved it for myself by saying that it is what the 'voice within' tells you. – Mohandas Gandhi

I want to carefully walk through some real examples on how to do this exercise because it is a bit tricky at first and yet getting good at this is a tremendously rewarding investment.

Case 1: Chris and *I don't like these jeans*

This one might make sense to many people. Chris contemplates wearing a pair of jeans. "But, I don't like these jeans," he muses. He notices that he is now feeling awful. That is step 1 – noticing.

As there is no outside stimulus that is causing a negative reaction, he is now certain that somewhere in the inner processing an untrue message just flashed.

Step 2: He takes his small notebook out and asks himself what he was just thinking about. *I just told myself I don't like these jeans.* He tests this statement. Does *I don't like these jeans* in itself feel bad, or is it an untrue statement? Does just that thought alone cause a problem? In his case, he decides no, the statement itself is pretty innocuous. Lots of times he finds himself not liking an item of clothing and this doesn't cause any particular reaction. So, *I don't like these j*eans is not the thought causing the negative feeling.

He has to go deeper now. He asks himself, what other thoughts, ideas, and beliefs are underneath the thought about the jeans. He finds that he also had a quiet part of him say *I look too skinny in those jeans.* The statement, *I look too skinny* (or too fat, or too short, or whatever) could be a neutral statement to some, but in his case it is not. Because, underneath *I look skinny* is another notion, *I am not attractive and I look bad*.

This statement does not feel very good to him; it causes a sinking feeling in his stomach. He goes deeper. Underneath, *I am not attractive* is this belief: *I am not attractive so I won't attract dates, and therefore love.* At the core he finds the belief, *I am not loveable*.

This is it. He may or may not like a pair of jeans, but this is not his emotional problem. He finds that somewhere inside of himself, he does not feel handsome enough to attract admiration, so therefore there is an inner message he is not good enough to attract love.

So, he has done step 2 and found the belief that felt bad. He knows that this means the statement *I am not attractive, so I am not loveable* **is not true**. It cannot be true; his 100% accurate indicator tells him that. So, something else must be true and now he has to find it.

> **I must re-emphasize here that the negative reaction is a 100% accurate signal that somewhere you are telling yourself something that is NOT TRUE.** That is what it indicates, and for this practice to work you must understand the 100% accuracy of the feelings generated.

Step 3 is to start thinking of and writing down statements that are more true by testing each new statement for a neutral feeling. Chris writes: *I am fine*. But, for him, this still causes a pinch, a bad feeling in his gut. The statement doesn't sit neutrally because a part of him doesn't believe this and so is resistant.

So, he tries again, *I am attractive but I feel unattractive*. This is better; it sits better, although it is not a perfectly calm feeling because he can still feel a thump in his gut when he thinks it.

He tries another: *Apparently I still am caught up in what the culture says is attractive and I tell myself that since I do not fit it, I am not good enough.*

This one sits fairly calmly. It feels fairly true. He adds: *I am still stuck on ideas of outward attractiveness as a measure of myself and I need to work on this.* By this time, this statement sits perfectly. He writes it down. Now, his inner symphony has a new message to play for him when this issue comes up.

Notice that a person's truth is very lengthy – several sentences long. This matches the fact that most individuals are complicated. You will find that your real inner truth will rarely be coined by a short, snappy phrase, so make sure you don't try to encapsulate what is true for you in too brief a statement.

Case 2: Sonia and *I will always feel this back pain*

Sonia explained that the statement "I will always feel this back pain – I will be in pain the rest of my life" makes her feel terrible; "But, I don't see how the exercise works because this idea would make most people feel unhappy, right?"

We started by looking at the statement itself. Is the idea, *I will always feel pain,* true? And if so, does it by itself cause a bad feeling? When we worked together to test it, the statement turned out to be not true because of the word *always.* Sonia did not actually know if her condition would be permanent. Right there, then, this was easy to spot. Thinking that pain is permanent was not actually true. So, it needed re-tuning.

She had to then turn the thought into something more true by using the neutral feeling test. She offered: *I might always feel this pain.* In her case, this truer statement caused some relief, although not perfectly calm and comfortable feelings. We continued testing statements for that neutral, non-disruptive sensation.

She eventually ventured this true statement for her self: *I do not want this condition to be permanent and it might not be. If it turns out to be, I will find ways to not let it ruin my life. It might take extra effort, but I will not let this condition or any other make me miserable forever.* This statement sat almost perfectly calmly when she checked it. The calm neutrality is her certain indication that this statement is true for her.

At this point, she had something that rings very true for her. If her spirits sink when thinking about back pain in the future, she will find her inner orchestra remembering this new tune more readily and singing it back more often.

I Promise You

I promise that you will also experience profound results from replacing old untrue beliefs and self destructive messages with actual truth. You will feel better, and think more calmly by this sorting, identifying and re-tuning process. You will also broadcast a more authentic you because of this clearer signal, one that is becoming more clutter-free and gunk-free every day. And expressing what is true for you leads us to Thing 2.

Key Points Summary

Thing 1 is to understand what is true for you, for the whole you.

You are complex and it is up to you to fully understand your complexities. This chapter asks you to visualize yourself as an orchestra that is broadcasting a symphony and your job is to listen to it.

Old assumptions and beliefs that are not true disrupt your symphonic composition and are often buried in the layers of your inner landscape.

The *Listening to Your Symphony* exercise is one way to find out more about your inner dialog:

- Pick a time when your feelings and/or thoughts seem really jumbled and you also have some time to yourself.
- Start with paper/pen or blank computer word processing page.
- You will allow each one of your inner parts, or voices, speak its peace in its entirety, one at time.
- You will write down what you are hearing from these parts of the symphony without editing or arguing.
- You will say: *Who is next?* And keep asking *Anything else?* until each one is completely finished.
- Keep going until there is no answer to *Who is next?*
- Absorb and remember the sensations when all the inner talk is quiet (this is the reward for your efforts)

The exercise, *Tune Up — The 100% Accurate Test for Finding What is True for You*, allows you to start sorting through any old false notions and beliefs and replace those with true ones.

Zings, hits, pops or sensations of negative reaction (that are not associated with an obvious stimulus) are a 100% accurate signal that you are digesting, or holding, or chewing on, or assuming, or believing, or processing, something that is NOT true.

The three parts of the *Tune Up* exercise are:

1) Notice the negative reaction.
2) Find what part of you was chewing on something not true by investigating and testing.
3) Replace that untrue belief with one that is really true for you by testing it and then writing it down for retention.

Make sure you know how to test for what is really true for you by testing the neutral, calm feeling a statement creates, whether you saying it to yourself or others.

Finding the belief that you are telling yourself that is not true is the key to clearing up your vibration.

Replacing untrue beliefs with true statements is important because it's this practice that creates the improved harmony of your symphony.

Some More Good Reads

The Astonishing Power of Emotions by Esther Hicks and Jerry Hicks

Feeling is the Secret by Neville Goddard (both 1944 and 2007 editions should work)

Chapter 7

Thing 2: What Music You Play

This above all – to thine own self be true,

And it must follow, as the night the day,

Thou canst not then be false to any man.

—William Shakespeare

Jamael is a soft-hearted 19 year old who is ready to walk away from his job because of the overwhelming stress he feels. "I'm the support pillar there, Margaret Ruth. If I don't do all the work, no one else will do it and the whole business will suffer." He adds: "I can't ask for a raise either; I really like the boss and want to be nice."

I explain that it would not be nice for the others if he left; it would be better for everyone if he stopped doing other people's jobs for them and feeling less stress at work. Then the boss could retain his best employee. But he can't imagine expressing himself honestly enough to make a change for the better. For Jamael, quitting is the natural response and the best solution to his problem. And so that is what he did.

You and I can continue to mask our feelings, tell white lies and say things that are not completely true to everyone. But if we do, we'll be forced to stop asking irrational questions such as: *Why can't I ever have a real relationship? Why can't anyone understand me?* and *Why does everyone in my life have trouble telling the truth?*

If we would very much rather have the best kind of relationships in our lives, we'll want to perfect the art of authentic, meaningful self expression. The second Thing to do in relationships is to be genuine. Our expressions need to convey what is true for us, allowing people to know who we really are and to trust us.

Plus, you'll find that sticking to your truth will also

eventually prove to be beneficial for your stress level. It is relatively easy to do – after you get better at it – and creates less angst and more reward over the long run.

I know this because *Seinfeld* taught me.

Universal Tenets and the Visionary Seinfeld

During the 1990s, The Great Seer and Wiseman Jerry Seinfeld illuminated and animated, *every Wednesday night on the American NBC television network,* a universal and comprehensive tenet concerning authentic and honest personal expression.

There is a famous *Seinfeld* episode where Jerry and Elaine, instead of explaining that they cannot understand her constant mumbling, pretend to hear what Kramer's girlfriend is saying by nodding, smiling and saying things like "yes!" Jerry ends up having to wear the Puffy Shirt on a possibly career enhancing *Tonight Show* appearance, causing hardship, angry feelings and embarrassment to everyone involved (in addition to contributing to the end of George's hand-modeling career).

These wise teachers revealed in profound and powerful ways a universal canon: *The initial small discomfort of communicating your real truth is NOTHING compared to the horrendous pain that occurs when the falsehood, little white lie or important omission backfires in your face.* Well, into their faces actually – but we all felt it.

Problems in Authentic Self Expression

When you say or do anything to please, get, keep, influence, or control anyone or anything, fear is the cause and pain is the result. – Byron Katie

I have clients who find the requirement of authentic expression the most difficult of the Three Things. Some folks have trained themselves over the course of their lives to not pick the most genuine personal response, but instead choose an expression based upon other criteria. These criteria are such things as considering of what other people will think or expressing what is the then loudest emotion or idea broadcasting in the inner landscape.

However, the second Thing necessary in close relationships is that you express yourself truthfully, authentically and meaningfully. Of course, self expression is an area full of landmines. Some main obstacles can be:

- Believing that what seems to be your truth will upset others
- Not really knowing how to express mixed feelings and uncertainty
- Bad cultural practices such as believing that you are supposed to be nice, tell little white/convenience lies, and always answer questions

Telling the Genuine Truth Means Listening to All of You (Not Just the Loud Parts)

Some people are afraid to reveal negative feelings and reactions such as being angry, mad or upset. Some are afraid that if they just blurt out their truth, they would be telling people all kinds of not very nice things as: *I hate you; That is an ugly dress; You're so dumb*. Many think these kinds of statements are "telling the truth!" And those can very well be honest reactions of someone.

However, *you* know something else. You know, after reading this far, that what is going on with you at any moment is more than just one persistent thought, one strident feeling or one overpowering emotion. You now know just because one part of you thinks or feels one way, it is entirely possible for another part of you to be thinking or feeling differently.

ISSUE BOX

Ack! Margaret Ruth,
I cannot imagine, running around just speaking my truth! What a disaster!

Perhaps it might be one if you are thinking of doing this for relationships that are neither personal nor close; that decision has the potential of causing some problems.

And perhaps it would be also a disaster if you only let the parts of you that are shouting the loudest at that moment dictate your reactions to others. As we have seen, the loudest voice in the inner orchestra is not always telling you the truth or speaking wisdom. So, yes, *only* expressing those parts of you could create terrible situations.

Say a person you know does or says something mean to you. This is not a perfect example as this book is about meaningful relationships and it seems unlikely that people who do this are worthy of a close, personal bond. However, suppose you are practicing truthful self expression when this occurs.

You initially experience a very angry reaction to what the person just did or said. If you are paying attention, and this comes from developing self awareness, you might then notice other reactions underneath the stage-hogging antagonism. You might, at the same time as you feel like lashing out, have all or some of the following going on:

- A part of you telling you to please stop talking to this person – it's been telling you this forever and you never listen.
- A part of you experiencing bitter disappointment that

someone would act like this after you have tried so hard.

- A part of you feeling compassionate at how messed up this person has become.
- A part of you wanting to analyze this poor person's problems.
- A part of you thinking about dinner.

All kinds of other things can be going on in the inner landscape that are quieter and not claiming center stage.

If there is only one reaction on all levels and that is something like *I am never talking to you again*, then there is your truth. Express that actual fact, if you feel like letting the other know.

On the other hand, if you have layers of different feelings about it, you do yourself a disservice by only perceiving one aspect – and the mean one at that.

In a perfectly self-aware case, the person's truthful reaction could be something like this: "My first response to you is anger and wanting to hurt you back. However, most of me just feels finished with this relationship and that part of me feels sad about that. That is where I am at right now. Give me a few more days and I will probably understand how I want to respond even better."

Ok, that is a bit much. However realize that if you are aware of all of yourself, your truth is usually not that bad. Perhaps it isn't what people want to hear. Perhaps what is true for you is that you can't make it, or you don't agree, or that a part of you is angry. It is rare that your real truth, reflecting the whole you, is going to be completely nasty or mean (that stuff is most often just one part of the whole).

Finding Ways to Honestly Reflect a Multidimensional You

> Seth: Affirmation means acceptance of your own miraculous complexity. It means saying "yes" to your own being. It means acquiescing to your reality as a spirit in flesh. Within the framework of your own complexity, you have the right to say "no" to certain situations, to express your desires, to communicate your feelings. – Jane Roberts

Many people think that telling their truth means having one quick and correct answer. If you have read Chapter 6, and recognized how complicated you are, you will understand how difficult it can be to distill all of that into one fast answer. An obstacle to genuine expression is that most of us do not allow ourselves the chance to notice the mixed feelings, the mixed reactions, the buried feelings or the hidden reactions.

For instance, Jessica is a client of mine who really could not get Thing 2 right. She was used to trying to be nice and staying positive no matter what else was going on. She was at that time deeply concerned over how her marriage was going. Although she was a mostly happy and positive person, she was also feeling strained from the internal worry and fears she was experiencing. And yet, she found herself telling partial truths, even to close friends — maintaining a mask of a preferred vision of Jessica perhaps — out of bad habit and a misunderstanding about the Three Things necessary for her personal relationships. She did not yet understand that being a complicated person meant finding ways to express mixed reactions and feelings.

This next exercise was one that helped Jessica, and others, practice being even more wholly authentic in their relationships.

Are you wondering about a situation where either you or someone else cannot tell the truth because of possible physical, emotional, or mental hurt? That person needs professional counseling and intervention immediately. People in potentially emotionally, physically, mentally destructive relationships need to get the utterly crucial issues of personal inner and outer health looked at by good professionals.

Honest Self Expression Practice

Try this exercise yourself. Take a week and just watch exactly how you interact, communicate and respond to others. See if you can pick up on times when you are not truly expressing yourself. This takes noticing your more subtle feelings and quieter parts of you. Don't judge yourself. For just the week, you are only going to get more skilled at *noticing what you do*.

For a second week, you will only express what is true. Take your time when talking with others; do not rush, even if that means the conversation passes you by. Try to find and then state what is going on with you in actuality. Practice saying things like the following suggestions (of course only if they are true):

I have mixed reactions
I don't know what I think
I'll let you know later
Most of me agrees with you, but some part of me is unsure.
I don't know what to say to that
That isn't a good time for me
I see your point, but I am feeling this other way right now
*I want to agree with you because you are my friend, but I really do
    not*

No, I do not feel fine about it but I will do it anyway

My first reaction is anger (or hope, or joy, or...), after that there are other reactions

I have a conflict and won't be there

I'd rather do it later

No, it is actually not one of my favorites, but I don't mind it

Oh! I just realized that I spoke so fast I didn't notice some additional reactions, so here they are too

My personal favorite, one I use constantly, is: *I'm having seven different reactions to that. I'll get back to you when I figure out the healthy one.* Try those and similar statements and let me know how you do.

For many, just getting permission to have complicated responses to ideas, events and conversations is enough to get them to start expressing that way. And then this all gets much easier with practice.

To Answer or Not to Answer? That is the Question.

There are a few other obstacles that come up when trying to tell your own truth. Most of these relate to being culturally trained to answer all questions rapidly or correctly, except for when they are uncomfortable and then we tell a little friendly fib.

Telling the truth is not the same as being required to answer every question ever thrown at you by anyone. Many of us revert to our school training to have the correct quiz answer on the tip of our tongues or to look clever because we know more than another. These are just bad habits. You can tell they are habits because not everyone does that. You do not have to answer everything asked.

For instance, responding to someone might be a waste of our time. There are cases where it is just easier to not say anything than have to deal with someone's argumentative state or stance.

Or, we perceive that our contribution is not necessary because the other is going to say whatever he or she was going to say no matter what we said.

Then there are times when someone asks a question and you just do not want to get into a discussion about the topic or with this particular person. Sometimes it is not any of their business. You have the choice to ignore someone if you want. You can change the topic if you would like.

There are also ways to be truthful if you wish it. Here are some handy sayings that can be used in such cases.

Thank you for asking. I appreciate it. (+you don't have to answer the question and can switch subject)

You are very considerate to think of me. (+don't answer the question)

What I like best about the present is that you gave it to me. So, because of that I treasure it.

I cannot thank you enough for that.

This is not a topic I enjoy. Let's talk about something else.

We argue about this topic and I am going to firmly avoid it.

Tell me what you think about it.

I'm not interested in talking about that.

I'm uncomfortable with discussing that right now.

What is the point of the question?

What is it you really want to know?

The key point is that you are not required to answer all questions; however, whatever you say, whatever you are expressing, must covey an authentic message from you.

White Lies or Little Lies of Convenience Do Not Really Work

Many of us have a bad habit of answering any question that gets posed to us, and then when we don't want to answer truthfully we have a white lie handy. White lies theoretically do not hurt anyone but they are harmful – for YOU. Additionally, this adds to broadcasting mixed messages, which does not help relationships in the long run. If this is not making sense to you, I refer you back to the Great Seer Seinfeld and his *Seinfeld* Seasons 1-7 DVDs.

Your genuine response to an emotionally loaded question like "Do I look fat in these jeans?" is usually going to be more than a yes or no (although those work fine too if they express your *full* truth), so don't fall back on bad habits of the little lies of convenience.

Sincerely honest replies that reflect what is fully true for you will be harder to generate at first, until you have developed the habit of getting to your core truth, but you still need to do it. People's entirely truthful response to such a complex question is usually more like these:

- I don't think you are fat – that is your issue – why would you ask me such a loaded question?
- When I look at you, all I see is wonderful. Why would ask me such a question?
- You know I don't think you are at a healthy weight – but that does not change how I feel about you.
- Your insecurity about your looks has nothing to do with me. I completely and already love you and do not want to be responsible for dealing with your insecurities. I want you to deal with them.
- I always think you look great unless you look tired, worn or stressed.
- Your weight means nothing to me and I am getting tired of

not being believed.

- What I hear you say is that you are feeling insecure about your looks – is that right?

Don't Lie. If you open your mouth to say something – whatever topples out must convey your real self.

How Much of This Truthful Expressing Am I Supposed to Do?

Sane and intelligent human beings are like all other human beings, and carefully and cautiously and diligently conceal their private real opinions from the world and give out fictitious ones in their stead for general consumption. – Mark Twain

You might be wondering where to draw the line between needing to tell your truth and not expending energy (and privacy) telling people stuff they don't need to know ("Too much information, man!"). There are no perfect guidelines for how much self revelation is necessary in your various personal connections, but here are some ideas to consider.

Pick only what is natural and real for you when it comes to choosing the quantity of personal expression. Because you are required to authentically express yourself, then how you do that must be your choice alone and you must choose what is happy and satisfying to you. If you prefer to be private, then that is right for you. If you are one who enjoys tons of self expression and self revelation, there you are.

Deciding further as to how much information you need to give another during an interaction depends on either what kind of feedback would be most helpful and/or what is needed to support your half of the particular connection. Convey information that affects the friendship/partnership with detail appropriate for the depth and nature of the relationship. There is no requirement for instance for you to communicate your truth to anyone you do not care to interact with on a personal level.

It does not seem mandatory that you must tell everyone everything about your thoughts, feelings and reactions. It does seem mandatory that, if something happening with you is impacting the particular relationship you have together, you communicate with the other person involved if you want to hold up your end in a healthy manner.

For instance, a spouse does not necessarily need to know every detail of your business trip. But, if you return exhausted and your tiredness interferes with your ability to hold up your relationship half, you would need to explain what is going on with you. On the other hand, a business partner probably needs to know all the business details of the trip and very little about your personal experiences.

How Should I Communicate All This Rampant Authenticity?

You and I can choose to handle our 50 percent of a relationship by being as proficient a communicator as possible, and I'm pretty sure that employing diplomacy where helpful is one of those perennially excellent ideas. Many people like framing their exchanges in ways that others can hear most clearly and therefore maximizing the possibility of being understood.

It seems to me that this is like throwing a tennis ball to someone. If you care about whether the other catches it – and remember you do not have to care, but if you do – then you might think about how it is thrown. You might consider the other person's frame of reference, vocabulary or language and decide to try to make your expression more comprehensible by your choices.

As you can imagine, here comes the big BUT. There exist perfectly satisfying relationships where the two involved are not necessarily great communicators, meaning they are not using well-selected words, language, expressions, modulations, volumes or even voice tones. It is then not always true that this is a necessary requirement of a perfectly satisfying connection.

ISSUE BOX

Hey MR – What about Good Communication?
Are you trying to say that all you have to do is tell the truth and not try to communicate well with your friend or partner? This doesn't sound very good.

I know that as I sit here typing away that it would be sort of silly of me to write these words and NOT think about expressing the ideas in an understandable way.

Just yesterday, I was trying to convey to my son Jim what I thought was a very important point about some paperwork of his. He really had no idea what I was getting at and why I kept hammering him. I could not understand why he did not see the crucial detail that needed handling.

Luckily, we have a solid HJW bond and know each other well enough to not get *too* cross with the other's rank obtuseness. I really floundered trying to explain my problem and kept trying to find ways to be understood. Knowing that your message isn't being understood is frustrating and explains why attempts at clear communications can be worth our time and effort.

I am happy to report though that neither of us thought to falsely act like we did get each other's point so to stay out of conflict, or to be nice, or to give the other what we thought they wanted to hear. This is the most important aspect of the interaction and the point of the chapter. At least I am clear on the fact that we did not communicate well. And that is important to know.

I am thinking of some couples I know who are evenly matched in being less than outwardly expressive; the couple I think of most often are two statisticians who have their own shorthand way of talking to each other. They might not qualify as adept communicators, but they understand each other and that seems to be all that is needed.

If everyone is perfectly satisfied, why change anything? It is false to assume that you need to be an expert communicator in order to have solid friendships and partnerships because we can find exceptions to that rule. On the other hand, beneficial communication skills can help – they can help quite a bit, quite often – but having them is not required.

In the case where you want to try to be understood, you can decide to become more aware of what words, tone of voice and body language you use. The key point though is that if you choose to express yourself, it needs to be true for you. *How* you do it is your personal choice.

Which Leads to the Third Thing

How others choose to express themselves is then their personal choice. You will be a relieved participant when you allow the others to hold up their end of the connection as they choose. It is metaphysically correct *and* less angst for you.

Key Points Summary

The second Thing to do is be genuine.

If you choose to convey information about yourself to friends and partners, it must be an honest and meaningful expression.

Great and Wise Seers have revealed that the initial small discomfort of communicating your real truth is NOTHING compared to the horrendous pain that occurs when the falsehood, little white lie or important omission backfires in your face. If we accept this universal principle for the conduct of close personal relationships, without having to experience these disasters for ourselves, our lives will be easier. *To not do this makes the teachers' efforts all for naught.*

Telling your truth requires listening to all of you, not just the loudest parts. If you only express the high-volume, stage-hogging constituents, it won't be wholly true for you and leads to miscommunication or, worse, unnecessary hard feelings.

When you become aware of all of your layers, expressing meaningful and genuine truths is usually not going to upset your close associates. Telling others things such as: "I cannot make it," "I'm not interested in this topic," and "I'm having five reactions to that," is not that hard to for others to hear.

Cultural training can make us feel like we have to answer all questions, correctly, with one nifty all-encompassing answer, and then avoid the difficult ones with small convenience lies (which are still a no-no even though they are easier at first). When it comes to sticking to your truth:

- Your truth does not have to be one perfectly correct one sentence phrase; you are not being tested or quizzed.
- Your truth is allowed to be mixed, such as having a mixed reaction, a mixed set of feelings, or being able to see the pros and cons of an idea.
- Your truth is allowed to be that you do not know, you do not know now or that you will not ever know.
- Your truth can be that you don't want to answer the question.

How Much: Identifying how much of your truth others need to know can be tricky, especially since people have different preferences for self revelation. One good rule of thumb might be to give others enough information to either support the particular type of relationship you share or get the kind of feedback you need.

How: Truthful personal expressions *can* include communication decisions that promote mutual understanding and many people find this a very satisfying way to hold up their half of a connection. The bottom line though is that how you express yourself is entirely your decision.

Further Good Reads

Being Genuine: Stop Being Nice, Start Being Real by Thomas d'Ansembourg

Dare to Be Yourself by Alan Cohen

Chapter 8

And Thing 3 Is Not Your Job

If I am not for myself, then who will be for me? And if I am only for myself, then what am I? And if not now, when? – Pirkei Avot 1:14

Kent had been ecstatically dating Michael for seven months but his pending overseas transfer prompted him to call the radio show: "This is the best romance of my entire life. But I get really upset about the future. Wouldn't it be better to break off now?" He undertoned, "I don't want to hurt him when I leave."

His relief from hearing my reply was palpable even across the airwaves: "Kent, there are only Three Things to do. You must figure out what is really true for you, speak honestly, and let him decide on his own. Very nice of you to be the daddy figure here and try to decide for everyone, but stop it. If Michael is a big boy, and my reading says he is, he will make up his own mind."

For this step, it is important to understand that you cannot do this step. What other people choose is out of your control. You have no responsibility for it. If you try to do this step, one that you actually cannot do, you will continue to struggle and find relationships hazardous to your health.

Picture your inner self again as the symphony orchestra. You have done your best to be self aware and develop a harmonious whole. You play your tune the best you can manage. That is all then. Just like a concert, the curtain comes down. The audience might applaud, throw tomatoes or do nothing at all.

However, at that point responding is not the performer's responsibility – it is the audience members'. So, when it comes to doing the third Thing, you know that after you play your best, a curtain comes down and you are done.

Here is another way to picture the Three Things:

1: Know what is true for you
2: Express what is true for you
Curtain down

If you have been hired to do a job, it's natural to be invested in, feel in charge of and attached to how employers respond to your work. That is why you are getting paid; it is in fact, yes, your assignment to produce something they will approve of.

On the other hand, if you are looking at your personal connections, this is not the case at all. You can choose to handle your end of a *personal* relationship by being as good a communicator as possible but you cannot be in charge of how others choose to react because that is their job.

There is an important difference between choosing an expression because it is authentic for you and choosing an expression because you are influenced by others' possible reactions. For some, these distinctions are practically impossible to discern. I've noticed that grasping the third Thing is challenging for three main reasons: 1) taking responsibility for how other people feel, 2) depending upon the others' reactions to feel good or 3) pre-deciding for others.

How to Correctly Do Thing 3 – Which Means Not Doing It

Unless we were rightly trained, or have untrained ourselves since, we tend to feel invested in, attached to and responsible for others' choices. We endeavor to get our friends to agree with us so we can feel good. Parents becoming upset with us seems to cause emotional upset within us. We decide that our mate won't like the Benicio Del Toro double feature, and so don't bother asking him to go.

It is perfectly reasonable to choose diplomatic language or a communication style that maximizes interpersonal understanding. What is a problem is changing the content of what is really true for you because of another's possible reactions. Examples are masking your emotions to make the other happy, indicating agreement without meaning it, telling someone what he wants to hear when it isn't really true and holding back something important so not to start an argument.

If this is an area you want to correct, you will need to notice when you alter your real expression because of others and then practice making others 100% responsible for their responses. When you get this job assignment right (Them = 100%, You = 0%), you will be amazed, and I am not exaggerating, at how much better you feel about your involvements with others. As difficult as Thing 3 may seem, it is worth extra attention.

The First Step Is to Notice

"What will they think of me?" – must be put aside for bliss.

– Joseph Campbell

You automatically know you are violating the third Thing when you are shielding, hiding, altering or changing your expression because of the other. Additionally, you can notice if any interactions cause you to feel more upset, worn, drained, angry, stressed, hurt or torn than before you had the exchange. We know that the negative feeling symptoms tell you that something is wrong, somewhere, and can often point to cases where you feel responsible for or dependent upon the others' reactions.

If you have double checked that you know what exactly is going on with you and that you communicated honesty, then if you feel some sort of upset during an interaction, you are either telling yourself something, somewhere, that isn't true or making yourself overly concerned with the other's reaction. Or both.

Another indicator to watch for is prefacing your statements with some kind of qualifier. Listen to yourself and catch anything like: "Now, don't get mad," "I don't want to upset you,"

"I need you to listen to me," "I want you to hear me out before you react," and "This isn't about you, it is about me." These kinds of statements, where you are prepping to get a different reaction than the usual, can be indications that you are invested in influencing the listener's reaction.

If you notice any of these signals, you were taking at least some responsibility for another's feelings, opinions, decisions, state of mind, reactions or behavior. And yet your actual percentage of responsibility for this = 0%; so you have a problem.

The Next Step is to Practice Not Being in Charge of or Attached to Others' Choices

The Dude: That's like...uh...like your opinion, man. – *The Big Lebowski* (film)

My client Jacob was always worrying about getting his wife upset. He found that he held back information or said things in vague ways so that she wouldn't dominate or argue with him. He couldn't imagine himself doing the third Thing with any competence; he loved his wife and felt extremely attached to her reactions to him. It helped him to have some visual or verbal stratagems to remind him that her choices were her job and not his.

You can try these, too. Think of a difficult person in your life whose interactions usually leave you with one of the negative feelings identified above; it could be a relative, a spouse or a friend. Decide you are going to practice the third Thing in these exchanges. However, don't pick a relationship that is too loaded with problems for the initial trials.

Before you call or talk to the person you have chosen, prepare yourself beforehand. Recall Thing 1 – know what is true for you. Do you have that ready?

Then, Thing 2 – express genuine truth. Do you know what you will say and how? You are ready to practice being not responsible for the response.

Say Jacob is truthful with his wife and says something like: "Sweetheart, this career (or church, or voting Green Party, or lawn care service) is not working out for me. I'm going to have to change something." Then, as she responds – whether with applause or tomatoes — Jacob can do something to separate himself from whatever her reaction turns out to be.

My favorite devices to get to this *not-in-charge-of-what-s/he-says* place are visualizations and verbalizations. Effective visualizations could be:

- You tune up. You play. Then a heavy red velvet curtain with extravagant gold fringe falls down between you and the audience. You are done.
- Your words or expressions leave you and go into a Black Hole of somebody else's choice of response.
- You throw the tennis ball, as best you can. You can try again if not caught. In the end, it is the other person's job to catch it.
- You express yourself and then the traffic light turns red for you. You put your foot on the brake and the other one gets the green. You are done because you can't drive another's car, only the other can.

Another helpful technique is to mentally sing a little song. I start one up when I find myself feeling upset, emotional or drained, indicating I am attached to or making myself the cause of what another decides to do.

While the other person is responding – either agreeing, happy, unhappy, critical – whatever it is, I sing a *100 -0, 100-0, That's their job, Not my job* sort of a tune. The main lyric while the other is handling his or her response is*: Not my job; Not my job.* My little humming keeps me remembering that once I have tried to explain things honestly and clearly, then I am done.

Another handy reminder chant is this one: "The person

*respon*sible for *respon*ding is the *respon*der." A bit too chipper for me, but might work for someone else.

When you finish saying what you want to say to the difficult person, I encourage you to find your own reminder – musical, visual, physical or verbal – that works to keep the boundaries clear and allows you to allow the other person to be responsible for the Thing 3 job.

People who get good at not being in charge of Thing 3 find that life becomes much easier when they no longer bear the unbearable burden of other people's choice of expression. So, as you get better at letting everyone around you be responsible for their reactions, your personal relationships become less stressful and easier to handle. You begin to enjoy them more and more.

Not being responsible for or in charge of others' choice of responses to your truth does not imply you don't care about what someone is saying.

What others say can be very important to you. Thing 3 means that what other people decide for their expression is their job and you do not control what others choose, so don't even try. You can listen to the others and care about what they say. You cannot, however, think you caused their reaction choice and you cannot let their reactions affect your self esteem (in either direction I might add) or how you feel about you.

There can be obstacles to getting to that sweet "not my job" space when it comes to the third Thing. The three main ones I've noticed are anticipating or deciding for others, feeling like how people react is your fault and depending upon others to make you feel ok.

Obstacle 1: Anticipating or Deciding for Others

There is a problem if you are pre-deciding for other people what their reactions might be and adjusting your communications because of that. Two issues come up around this: deciding for people without their input and acting for them and changing your truth because of your anticipation of their reaction.

> **Jill:** He asked me out in the email, but I am not sure I should take him up on it. I wonder if he was just being polite or something like that.
> **Beverly:** Just name a time when you are available and that is convenient for you. If he takes you up on it, he wanted to do it. Otherwise, he didn't really. Don't try to guess for him.
> **Jill:** Geesh - what was I thinking? You're right.

Jill almost trapped herself by trying to figure what the other person really wanted and meant, thus making a decision for him, and thus affecting how she communicated.

If you have ever been in a relationship where the other person kept thinking for you and making decisions based on his conjecture of what you would want, you will understand these examples of people thinking for the other.

Example 1: Deciding that you cannot invite both of two friends to an event because they don't get along. This is very wrong – it is their decision as to whether or not to come. You would tell them both the truth, which is that you want them there, and let them decide

Example 2: Thinking you will not go out with someone, whom you like, because the other person will not approve of your ___ (fill in the blank: religion, politics, dress code, tattoos, military affiliation, poetic nature) ___ . This is very wrong - that is his/her decision as to whether or not dating you might be enjoyable.

Example 3: Not inviting people over because you do not want them to think your domicile is __ (fill in the blank: too expensive, too cheap, too shabby, too fancy) __. This is very wrong – that is their decision (or problem). If they would like to be judgmental about your very fancy or very run-down home, that is their business.

Example 4: Having a question about how someone feels or thinks about something, then making up your own mind as to what they would want, and then proceeding to ____ (make the plans, go ahead without them, not make the plans, cancel flights, cancel concert tickets, get tickets)__.

Okay this last one was personal. I once had a boyfriend who was constantly pre-thinking what would or would not work for me and then acting on it. Very sweet, very paternal – and extremely unnerving (mostly because he was usually wrong).

Obstacle 2: Feeling In Charge of Others' Choices and Absorbing Their Stuff

> We will discover the nature of our particular genius when we stop trying to conform to our own or to other peoples' models, learn to be ourselves, and allow our natural channel to open. – Shakti Gawain

My sister Bonnie announced recently that she has decided to not take anyone's crap anymore (this is a direct quote). This was her New Year's Resolution, and a fine one it was too.

Me: This is a real disappointment to me, Bonnie, because I will now have to find someone else upon whom to unload all my crap. This is VERY *inconvenient for me.*

Bonnie: *Oh well. Too bad.*

Becoming aware that it is unhealthy to allow anything anyone might want to toss at you – so now you can hold it – is a terrific start towards dissolving self-assigned responsibility for what is going on with others and for how they are acting. Some folks go so far down that particular road that they choose to believe they are at fault if, when expressing themselves honestly, someone else gets upset or mad at the communication.

Tasha and Geno hated going to their father's house. He was unpleasant, negative and a perpetual invalid. Staying away too long encouraged their father to make them feel guilty for the neglect. Being at the house too long was miserable as they had to watch everything they said so he would not start shouting. In their minds, they had to act in ways that were not honest for them in order to maintain the relationship.

The dynamic was set so that whenever they said or did something that upset their father, Geno and Tasha were unconsciously taking responsibility for how their father acted. They let their father's issues and reactions become their own, and affect their own well being by *absorbing his stuff* or *carrying his stuff for him*. In this case, the father was able to make others accept blame for how he acted and we have to be certain that this diminished any incentive to change.

Of course, they can just keep walking on the proverbial eggshells around him into the foreseeable future and resign themselves to having a less than satisfying relationship. However, as long as they keep forgetting the 100-0 Law and the necessity of not-doing Thing 3, they are going to continually feel miserable about interactions with him.

And that is true for all of us. Holding people's stuff for them, or taking on their issues and problems as if these were also ours, is very detrimental to not only you but to them. I featured a fancy *Prime You* picture in Chapter 2. I want to render it even fancier now.

The *Prime You* showed your optimal condition as an inviolate self with the good boundary. If this picture gets magnified some more, I can indicate how the boundary needs to let most of the stuff that people throw at you bounce off.

The optimal personal boundary does not allow absorbing other people's negative issues or anyone's problems as your own.

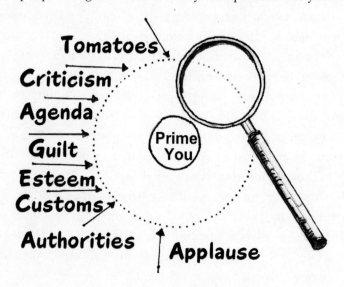

More Prime You

It is best for everyone if you do not absorb, put up with, agree to or join with their unhealthy emotions, harmful behavior, negativity, baggage, hurt, anger and defensiveness.

First, to be willing to support, by action or inaction, negative attitudes, behaviors or feelings keeps the troubled person from acquiring important information. For Geno and Tasha to just nod their heads, allow the verbal abuse and accept guilt for their father's discomfort did not help him find real ways to feel better.

Further, if you digest any part of someone else's negative condition, feelings or situations as your own, that person has less motivation to figure out his stuff because his burden just got lighter when you took some on. If I were to fight all of my friend's fights for him, he wouldn't have much motivation to either stay out of them or find his own way to solve them.

Many of us know that sometimes we need to shoulder some

extra burden on behalf of our close ties, but ready assistance does not require absorption and infiltration past your good boundary. My friend Andie verbalizes her boundary using statements such as: *That's not mine — that's yours; That's your issue; That belongs to you.* When she does this, both people in the relationship can remind themselves of whose stuff is whose.

ISSUE BOX

Margaret Ruth – You Imply We Can't Help Others!
What if my loved ones are suffering? What about someone in crises? You imply we are to detach from them! To not help?

There is always someone who is HORRIFIED about the third Thing and especially over this idea of not being allowed to take on other people's stuff as their own.

The misunderstanding that needs to get cleared up and the key point I need to establish is that helping and offering assistance is different from feeling responsible for how others feel and react, which is essentially absorbing or taking on their stuff.

The best clue to how to effectively help others and maintain healthy boundaries might come from the healing professions such as psychotherapists, doctors and nurses. Healing professionals know they cannot assign themselves responsibility for patients' choices, or they wouldn't be able to keep doing their jobs.

What we can do for other adults – and you can do this all the time whenever you like without diminishing your self – is be someone's best cheerleader, greatest pat on the back, wise advisor and committed friend. We can offer all the mental, physical, emotional and financial help we can

---

honestly give without hurting our own self.

What we cannot do is mess up the boundary and cross that line where we are feeling it for them. If you are someone who does this, understand that you must love them enough to let them own it themselves. If you continually take on stuff that isn't yours, you will experience some negative personal results, such as those discussed in Chapter 3.

Thing 3 requires us to absolutely avoid absorbing anybody else's thoughts, emotions, energy or vibe – without giving it a once-over and deciding it is interesting, informative, fun or helpful.

Obstacle 3: Needing Approval from Others

I was always looking outside myself for strength and confidence, but it comes from within. It is there all the time. – Anna Freud

Take a moment now, look within and ask yourself some questions about self worth and self-approval. On a scale of 1-100, how important to you is getting approval from others such as spouses, mates, parents, relatives and friends? How important is approval from professional and impersonal associates? Do you care more about what others say about you then what you think about you?

What does the word *approval* mean to you? What does it mean if someone *approves* of you; does it mean you are liked? Admired? Agreed with?

Add ideas and questions of your own. Find out what the issue of approval means to you in a real, honest and deep way.

Go within again. Discover what needs to happen in order for you to be perfectly self approving and feel like a worthy person. What exactly do you need from others in order to approve of yourself? What overt symbols or attainments do you need to feel like you are a worthy person? How would you feel if you approved of you but no one else did?

Most people who do this thought experiment cannot quite come up with a mechanism to become perfectly self-approving; it can be especially difficult to find a way of self-affirming that does not depend upon outside validation.

It seems just natural to some (but not all) that their personal expression must be designed for others' approval. This other-based training is characterized by thinking that you need to fit in, worrying about what others will think, needing others to agree with you, finding self esteem only when others compliment you and wanting everyone to like you.

Sheer logic dictates that being so dependent sentences you to a lifetime of unhappiness. The real and relentless and utter truth is that no amount of people standing around and approving of you can *make* you feel good about yourself. Only you can do this because the 100-0 Law is immutable. So, it is humanly impossible to ever get enough self-esteem through other people's opinions and reactions.

In the end, you must be able to see that the only approval you ever need is your own and the only person who can decide what is good enough is you. And because this is a tough area, I have a very useful exercise on getting at the part of you who refuses to acknowledge that you are already perfect (even in your imperfections).

Note from Margaret on Wanting Others to Like You

Realize that most people can count on two hands their amount of, what they would consider to be, real and satisfying bonds. Do not get nervous or upset because you do not have many very close friends. They are a rare commodity when compared to the number of your acquaintances or casual friends. This is because the amount of people who will actually understand you is rather less than the amount of population you will meet up with.

The more you like and understand yourself, the less you will require others to like and understand you. This is an absolute and sure result; anyone who has progressed through this self-affirming and awareness process will be able to verify this *certainty* for you.

The corollary of this of course is that anyone who obsessively craves others to like her/him will have a fair amount of inner insecurity, weak boundaries and a poor self concept. This is Bad.

Exercise: *Good Enough*

It is much easier to become the best decider of your own worth when you locate and correct the parts of you that tell you that you are not ok and you are not good enough. The exercise of *Good Enough* is worth trying as it can be very effective for getting past needing others' approval because it allows you to start approving of yourself.

In Chapter 6, there was an exercise called *Listen to Your Symphony*. It had you take some time to record all the various parts of you and the things they say at any one time. Start this exercise again.

Close you eyes and focus on your inner self. Tell the jumble of ideas, thoughts and voices you will be going through them one at a time. Ask now: Who is first? Remember, the first voice is often a very loud, fearful, critical or mean sort of voice, especially if you pick a confused, upsetting time to do the exercise. You say to it: Anything else? What next? Keep going until it is completely finished.

Watch for the fearful, mean, critical part of you. When that one is finished talking, stop there and start talking to it. Some people call this inner dialoging or inner voice therapy. The important aspect is that You, with the capital Y, talks to that critical part of you.

The script I have below is quite effective as it closely matches what goes on when I am meeting live with someone. Use it or any others that work even better for you.

You begin by saying this: *"Ok, my mean, critical voice. What you are saying to me is that I am really bad, have these flaws, and do things wrong. Essentially I am not good enough. Is that correct?"*

It (that voice of the mean self) usually responds with something like: *"Yes, that is correct."*

You: *"Ok – you win. I will now do everything you say. Tell me, when will I be good enough? What exactly do I have to do to be good enough? Tell me and I will do it."*

Here I have you pause and listen for the answer, from *that part of you only* – not from your nicer parts, just this mean one. Write down what it says about what you need to do in order to be *good enough*. Two possible rejoinders occur at this point. One is that it tells you what it wants you to do to be *good enough*. Or, and this is most typical, it has *No Answer* to this at all. Sort of a big, drafty, echoing internal silence follows the request.

Next, I will have you pin this mean voice down with concrete examples of what might make you *good enough*. You will ask it if you attain these examples, then will you be *good enough*? The key is to get that part of you to describe precisely what has to be earned or done for it to deem you *good enough*.

Assume your inner mean voice says that you have to "get a good job, finish school and put money in the bank," in order to be *good enough*. Follow up with this (do not stop here, you will see why in a moment).

You: *Ok, you are saying that the day I get a Good Job, Finish School, and Have Money in the bank, is the day I will be good enough?*
It: (*Silence*)
It: *Well, not really*

Now the real dialoging begins. I have you now think of the most extravagant things you can that seem very special, or prestigious, or famous, or something that would seem like large successes. Then, insist that the It, or the mean inner voice, answers you when you give it scenarios. Here is a possibility (go wild with this, by the way).

You: Ok. *I see. According to you, that really won't be enough to be good enough. Here's a scenario. What if I earn two doctorate degrees, make the cover of Vogue magazine and get elected to public office? Will I be good enough on that day?*
It: (listen and see what it says, then keep going)
You: *Ok. Still not good enough. How about if I am the world's top movie star, write a best -selling novel, and become a billionaire? Will I be good enough on that day?*
It: (usually about this point it says something like the following): *Well, that is pretty good, but you are still not quite.*

And keep going. You will find, if you are having trouble mastering Thing 3, that no matter what impressive scenario you pose for your critical self, you will not be *good enough*. So, here is how you end this script and exercise. At this point, you will want to write it all down, if you have not already.

I want you to finally end with the following statement (and stick pretty close to this):

You: *Since, according to you, I cannot do, achieve, be or get* *anything that will make me good enough, at any point in time, I am going to have to ask you to not chime in anymore unless you have something constructive to add or suggest. From now on, I going to make decisions for myself based upon what seems the most fulfilling, most joyful and most rewarding choice. Are we copasetic? Thank you for your input.*

When, at some future point, you notice that part of you criticizing you, complaining or being mean, repeat this exercise. The process will get easier and faster each time you try it. The payoff is worth the effort; over time, *It* gets quieter and quieter as you repeatedly show *It* to be a hollow, information-less part of the orchestra. This is always the case; you can count on that.

Key Points Summary

There is a huge difference between choosing what you express for your own purposes and choosing what you express using others' purposes as your guide. That is the distinction to constantly be aware of as you make these choices.

Identifying times when you change your own expression because of someone's possible reaction can help you stop this unhealthy pattern

Because of the 100-0 Law, Step 3 is not your job in a relationship; it is the other's job to react to your truth. Visualize a curtain coming down or sing the "Not my Job" song to yourself to get you out of the habit of being responsible for others' choices of expression.

It is important to develop a firm awareness of and commitment to not feeling responsible for others' reactions because it is impossible to be so.

Pull back from thinking or pre-deciding for others and allow them to do their own thinking and deciding.

Allowing others to impact your sense of self worth or self-approval by their behaviors and reactions is not going to ever really work well.

The exercise of *Good Enough* is effective in quieting some of your most critical inner voices, which helps release you from needing outside validation of your worth.

Further Good Reads

Codependent No More: How to Stop Controlling Others and Start Caring for Yourself by Melody Beattie

The Four Steps to Wisdom by Anthony de Mello

Chapter 9

Then Flip It for Thing 3*

Josie: We can't change who he is. Not without dropping him in a vat of toxic waste. – *Sky High* (film)

Complaint, Margaret Ruth. So far it seems that completely focusing on yourself is the way to have relationships. That does not make much sense. There is another person involved – you have to think about the other!

If you want a two-way connection and a mutual bond, then there is a very, very, very good time to think about the other person; it just isn't when you are doing Thing 1, Thing 2 and not doing Thing 3.

Let's flip the direction, and now you are the on the listening side, the receiver of what others are broadcasting. I want to specify the responsibilities of everyone on that end of the interaction. The Things that others have to handle for their half of the relation might be called 1*, 2*, 3*. The other people's jobs might be summarized like so:

1* Know what is true for them
2* Express themselves truthfully
3* ~~Your response to their truth~~ not their job

When others are relating and communicating, here is how your responsibilities break down:

1* ~~Know their truth~~ –0% your responsibility
2*- ~~Speak their truth~~ 0% your responsibility.
3* Your response is 100% your responsibility because they have no real control over you

The Complete Picture: Your Three Responsibilities

If the intent is to enjoy enriching, meaningful and healthy relationships, we now have everything necessary.

If the aim is for something less, then the model, the rules, the road map and requirements for less healthy and inauthentic types get geometrically more complicated and convoluted (and, recall, not covered here).

Viewing the Three Things from the other direction makes it clear that our job is to choose what kind of response we make to the other person. For the complete exchange then, here is the final division of who does what when establishing meaningful, personal connections:

Your responsibilities in conducting personal relationships are:

1 Knowing your whole truth (every note in the composition)
2 Expressing your genuine self
3* Responding to others' expression

These are not yours:

1* Others' level of self awareness
2* Others' choice of expression
Others' choice of response to your truth

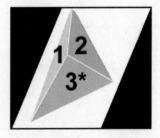

All the Pieces

Even if you do not agree with the assumptions this book has

developed (for some odd reason), you have to agree that sticking to the parts of your relationship that are strictly your responsibility is much easier and less stressful, once you get into the habit, than other choices you could make. You will spend no energy trying to control or pre-decide how others will choose to think and act. You will spend your time considering what is true for you, how to express it in a way that is authentic and then assessing what is best when you respond to others' expressions.

Be Conscious of What You Are Choosing for Thing 3*

It takes two to speak the truth — one to speak, and another to hear.

– Henry David Thoreau

If you are willing to know what is true for you and express that authentically, the beginning of a connection forms when another hears, understands or takes interest in what you are honestly communicating.

It begins when another metaphorically and actually tunes into your broadcast. The flip side of that is also true and the response chosen impacts whether a possible connection can begin. So, if you respond to others, which is your 100% *responsibility*, make sure you are doing what you intend to do.

Here are some possible choices of reaction to someone else's transmission, along with a likely result of the choice.

Your Response	Possible Result
1. Ignore	No Connection
2. Be Non-responsive	No Connection
3. Change the Topic	No Connection
4. Seek the Limelight	No Connection
5. Switch to Own Agenda	No Connection
6. Indicate Interest	Connection
7. Indicate Understanding	Connection
8. Ask for Clarification	Connection

9.	Smile and Nod	Connection
10.	Encourage	Connection
11.	Debate	? Depends
12.	Disagree	? Depends
13.	Manipulate or Try to Alter	Anti-connection

The first five listed are reliable choices for when you are not really interested in establishing a relationship. They would be indicators to the other person that you are not interested in hearing more or understanding more. There can be many good reasons for such, so those reactions are useful.

Note, by choosing something similar to the first five options, you are signaling that what another is expressing is not meaningful or something you want to pursue and have chosen not to connect. If you do this to a partner, relative or friend continually, the bond will weaken. And at that point, no one will listen as you woefully lament your lack of real relationships.

Options 6-10 look like positive choices if you want to connect with a person because these all indicate that you were listening to what s/he was expressing and, at a minimum, are interested enough to get more details.

The next two are toss-ups because your disagreeing with someone does indicate that the speaker was heard – the important issue – and sometimes that is effective. Other times, depending upon how the debate exchange is handled (see below), it might not work.

In all of that you want to remain authentic. Although you want to be conscious of the response you choose, it still must express what is true for you.

Finally, if you try to alter someone's genuine expression, something that is really true for the person, you create something akin to an anti-connection. Examples are such responses as "Don't feel like that," "Everyone else is doing it," and "You are *stupid* to think that (or *horrible* or *selfish* or whatever epithet gets tossed in there)."

Depending upon the history between you two, an attempt to manipulate something that is true for another can cause the other to feel anything from plain anger to multitudes of conflicting emotions, hardly any of those good. This is because doing that creates a push against another's broadcast and is like trying to take over someone else's symphony. It violates the universal condition that each unique consciousness is sacrosanct and, of course, breaks the 100-0 Law and all its corollaries.

Developing and Strengthening Your Connections to Others

Friendship is born at that moment when one person says to another, "What! You too? I thought I was the only one." – C.S. Lewis

Wanting to develop an association often happens when another person's qualities appeal to you and you would like to know him/her better. There are also situations where you would like to improve a relationship with a neighbor, co-worker, family member, boss or client. Just think too, there will even be parties where you are talking about adorable dogs, someone smiles and agrees, and you want to connect back.

The most direct and easiest way to consciously bond with others is to get on their wavelength or tune in; this means to hear, understand, accept or take interest in what they are communicating. It is pretty simple and not very easy to do. There are times when we are so concerned about what we are going to say next or how we are being perceived there seems little room left to focus on what another person is communicating.

There are many ways to relate. Understanding another person can mean asking questions, seeing his point of view, getting the joke or relaying similar experiences of your own. Asking for clarification indicates an interest in understanding the other. Even disagreeing might do it since it indicates that you listened and are interested in what is being said. Other supportive reactions can be:

Dude – you rock.
Hey, that was good.
You like Dogs? Me too!
I understand that.
How do mean that?
Why do you feel that way?
Yeah (or Yah or Yup depending upon region)
I love it when that happens!

In addition, reflection is a well known rapport building technique that can be effective. Doing it moves the listener closer to the other's psychic wavelength, and this is the bottom line of what needs to happen metaphysically for links to form.

Reflection is basically recounting what you believe the other person is saying, feeling or conveying. If I tell you I am hungry, a reflection would be: "If I understand you, you want to eat now?" Responses are usually questions, although not always:

You seem tense
Let me understand this, you said.....
So – you are saying...
If I understand you correctly, you feel...
You look happy
You are throwing off mixed messages; your body language signals bored but your face is smiling.

Reflection, because it also helps to catch misinterpretations, can be very effective in keeping channels clear between two people; you might want to add this to your arsenal.

Electric Connections

I am a proponent of the Electric Connections formed via the World Wide Web. It helps the musicians and poets gather the audiences that appreciate them. It helps people with off-beat interests and hobbies share with like-minded souls. People looking for spiritual or intellectual brethren can now find these easily.

For instance, I could go for weeks around my current home town and not meet one person who has read the Seth books from author Jane Roberts. However, I can connect to her readers across the globe through multiple forums and internet groups and thus enrich my life experience, something I have done and it has made my life better.

Many others, and possibly you too, experience great satisfaction in being able to make connections this way. And being perfectly satisfied is what we want to feel about our personal ties.

Some propose that these electric connections are not as good as in-person connections. Perhaps not. In instances where there are no opportunities to physically meet up, being able to bond electrically is a wonderful next best option. Being able to do this assists many in understanding that they do not have to try to fit in with just those in the geographic vicinity.

So, I am basically espousing the idea that forming connections based upon shared intellectual, emotional, creative and spiritual, albeit electronic, grounds can be healthy and rewarding for many – as long as they still know to do the Three Things electronically also.

Those techniques can also help to complete a connection. Say you are at the party from Chapter 5 where someone tuned in to you and created an opening by saying she liked dogs too. You can link back by reciprocating. Your 3* choice could be something like this:

Why do you like dogs?
Do you have any dogs?
Got any good dog stories?
What's your name?

With such responses, the circuit is complete. When people share enough of these small links, and/or the connections get repeated, a stronger bond with each other develops. If they come to accept and acknowledge each other just they way they are, the bond can become meaningful and authentic.

Two people can become friends, good friends, best friends, romantic partners and life partners. And, these relationships almost always begin with the first positive click.

The Remaining Untrue Stuff Restated to Actual Truth

It is not our purpose to become each other; it is to recognize each other, to learn to see the other and honor him for what he is. – Hermann Hesse

We're done constructing the book's five piece framework, including the Three Things, for developing perfectly satisfying relationships. It seems to me a good idea at this point to roundup the remaining untrue relationship beliefs we bumped into along the way and make sure these get corrected into true statements.

Not True: *Fitting in is good.*

Yes – if we lived in a wolf pack. But we don't, despite rampant confusion about that.

Fitting in is good for team situations, such as the armed forces, where it is important that the group's objectives dominate our search for an authentic individuality – and there isn't anything wrong with group efforts. However, the Three Things do not apply to groups and teams because these are not interpersonal relationships.

True Restatement: *It can be beneficial to fit in at times, but it is not good to make fitting in more important than expressing who you really are in your personal relationships.*

Not True: *It is important to be well liked.*

It is important to some people to have many friends. It is important for some people to be popular and well regarded. However, these statements do not apply to everyone. There have been important renegades, hooligans and mavericks throughout history that were not very well liked at all and yet lived full, satisfying (to them) lives.

So, unless you are dependent upon ratings to survive (which would then be a TV or radio show business and not applicable to personal relationships), you can live a very fine existence with hardly any one liking you at all.

True Restatement: *It is not mandatory to be well liked or have a lot of friends; some people enjoy that and some people don't need it.*

Not True: *In order to like yourself, you need others to like you.*

The counter evidence to this statement is that there are many, many people around that are well liked, but do not feel good about themselves.

There are also some that are the opposite; they feel good about themselves without having many others like them. So, we know that the statement above is not always true.

True Restatement: *The real key is to not find yourself by making people like you but rather make you like yourself, and then find like-minded people.*

Not True: *Being your self isn't always a good idea.*

This is similar to a common belief that goes something like this: *If I want people to like me, I have to __(fill in the blank: be nice, flatter them falsely, agree with them, bite back on my opinions, pretend to be too cool for the scene, play dumb)___.* However, being your self is mandatory for any situation where you want to develop fulfilling connections with the others.

True Restatement: *If someone doesn't get or isn't ok with your genuine self, do you have any business trying to have a close relationship with that person?*

Not True: *Playing games is inherent in relationships.*

True Restatement: *Healthy, Joyful, Whole relationships are impossible to create with falsehoods and dishonesty.*

ISSUE BOX

But wait Margaret Ruth!
The model doesn't explain how to make people want to be friends with me. I still don't know how to get others to like me back!

I hear you. We'll focus on that one more time.

We'll Finish Up with the Topic of *Getting People to Like Us*

One underlying fear of facing disapproval, disinterest or nonacceptance is that we will be not liked by the people we like. This is not that weird. It is pretty standard to want the people we like to reciprocate, and also it is not unusual to like someone who does not feel the same way. That happens to every person and so does not mean that you and I are unlikable.

It just means that we don't have a link with that individual and a mutual connection cannot happen at that point in time. There will be situations where no matter how effective a job you and I do as the responder, choosing the best 3* we can, there isn't enough affiliation.

When you feel discouraged about getting someone to like you back, there are a few points to remember. Recall that all the healthy, joyful, whole people are all running around with each other; remind yourself that *like connects to like*.

The other person involved might be on a different HJW playground than you are. If so, you can figure out if you want to change playgrounds (But *only* if it's a Healthier, Happier playground).

Next, make double sure that you like, appreciate and understand your self first – even your goofy parts. It keeps you from needing others to fill a hole in you and also broadcasts a clearer signal. Instead of transmitting mixed messages of "I need you to like me so I can like myself," which is frankly logically inconsistent, you will send a true "I like me and it's lovely if you like me too, but I don't need it" vibe.

However, it is very hard in actuality to always feel okay when someone doesn't like us. If you still feel bad or sad about someone not accepting or appreciating you, feel your feelings and announce these two truths firmly to your self:

1. *This bad reaction means that* somewhere *inside I am telling myself* something *that isn't true and I pledge to find it.*
2. *I further recommit to accepting and appreciating myself 100% from now on because not doing so feels very bad.*

And Finally, I Do Not Care About What *They* Think

And I ask you to do all this because I don't want you to care if the others like you or not. I want you to care terribly about whether *you* like you or not. I want you to care terribly about what *you* think about your Self. I want you to care deeply about how *you* feel, who *you* are and what *you* want. I want you to ardently, ferociously, passionately care about doing your actual real job: living your life to the fullest.

I only care that people in your life appreciate who you really are, as you are.

If I could pick, I would whisk anyone unable to do this clean out of your vicinity and into the remote-hinterlands called *Just Acquaintances,* and so allow more room for future people who *can* appreciate you.

If I could pick, you wouldn't allow anyone to do anything at any time that undermines your well-being.

If I could pick, you would care so powerfully about your freedom to be an authentic you that nobody on the planet will ever be able to inflict personal opinions upon your core self image.

And, under no circumstances do I want you to walk away from this book believing that what other people think of you needs to affect you too much.

All that above is what I care about and I will do everything I can think of to get you to care about that too. So this is what I will attempt now in the time we left together.

Key Points Summary

Your responsibility in conducting relationships is these Three Things:

1 – Knowing your whole truth

2 – Expressing yourself truthfully

3* - Responding to others' choice of expression

That's it. That is what you are responsible for in relationships. The rest belongs to the others.

These steps are 0% your responsibility in relationships:

Step 1* - Others' level of self awareness and personal truth

Step 2* - Others' choice of expression

Step 3 - Others' choice of response to your truth

You can choose to make, keep, begin, maintain or complete a connection with another – or not. The others can do the same, choose to connect – or not.

We all feel connected when another indicates interest, enjoyment, understanding or acceptance of our authentic expression.

An *untrue-beliefs* last roundup identified more false ideas and re-stated these into true relationship statements to memorize:

- *Healthy, Joyful, Whole relationships are impossible to create with falsehoods and dishonesty.*
- *If someone doesn't get or isn't ok with your genuine self, do you have any business trying to have a close relationship with that person?*
- *It is not mandatory to be well liked or have a lot of friends; some people enjoy that and some people don't care at all.*
- *It can be beneficial to fit in at times, but it is not good to make fitting in more important than expressing who you really are in your personal relationships.*
- *The real key is to not find yourself by making people like you but rather make you like yourself, and then find like-minded people.*

And finally, Margaret Ruth only cares that you fully like yourself and is fairly disinterested in other people's opinions about that.

Some Further Good Reads

How to Win Friends & Influence People by Dale Carnegie

Emotions Revealed, Second Edition: Recognizing Faces and Feelings to Improve Communication and Emotional Life by Paul Ekman

Chapter 10

Find Exciting New Things about You Using Mirrors

We meet ourselves time and again in a thousand disguises on the path of life.

– Carl Jung

Maria was grave: "I wanted to ask if I need to get a new group of friends. They don't seem to respect me. They don't seem to give me credit for my business accomplishments. I wonder if they are healthy for me."

"Keep your friends; they are doing you a great favor," I told a startled Maria. "Who is it that needs to respect you more? Who is it that doesn't give herself enough credit? Who is it who questions her value? Let them keep mirroring what you still need to do for yourself. When you have reached the point where you wholeheartedly respect and appreciate yourself, you won't be bothered by this issue."

She completely understood this. Good for her.

Why can you ignore some advertisements but cannot resist paying attention to others? The irresistible ones are pushing a button and some feeling or reaction flares up from the stimulus. Some appeals are clear; the message conveys heightened joy or fear and your attention antenna picks up those highlights.

For instance, if we worry that others won't be attracted to how we look in jeans, advertising that scares us into buying its amazingly-attractive-jean-product exploits these fears. This can be very persuasive (if we aren't conscious of the manipulation).

If no one pays attention to an ad, it is unsuccessful. Indifference and feeling neutral to the stimulus, such as being able to ignore some advertising, indicate absence of heightened response to the ideas, products or people on display.

Truly being indifferent to someone is worse for them than active dislike and explains why some people crave any kind of attention, even negative.

There are energetic reasons for this. As we saw in the last chapter, it is the act of attending to the other that can create a link. No dual links exist where all attention is withdrawn on one side. This is also referred to as giving someone, or something, no energy.

In addition, *saying* we are indifferent is not the same as actually *being* indifferent, which would entail detachment on all of our various parts and levels. We all know someone who swore He Was Done with That Other Terrible Person but the fact that he never stopped talking about that reputed horrible person revealed quite the opposite.

Just like ads that catch your interest, the heightened emotions that your personal bonds create generate heightened attention. Heightened emotions and attention can generate heightened self-perception.

So if you choose, your relationships can continue to be powerfully self-revelatory. And I think you will recognize that the closer the relationship – physically, emotionally, mentally and spiritually – the stronger the reactions, and therefore the more you can learn about your self.

Every Relationship Has a Mirror

He who knows others is wise. He who knows himself is enlightened.

- Tao Te Ching

Every relationship has a mirror where you can explore your self at as deep a level as you allow the relationship, and you, to go. If you are someone committed to becoming healthy, joyful and whole, then acute awareness of your reactions will rapidly advance progress down this path. Close associations are the most potent feedback system as they have the capacity to stir up our emotions almost more than anything else.

The key to swift progress is to interpret this feedback – your reactions – correctly. Instead of using relationships as a crutch whereupon to hang either one's self worth (that always works well) or insecurities out to dry (that's fun too), realize our heightened reactions are really pointers towards self discovery.

These reactions may not contain data about the other person at all. Re-envisioning the meaning of your relationship reactions as information about you, instead of about the other, is one of the most calming and rapid methods to gain personal clarity.

What other people are doing or expressing will cause a roughly positive, neutral or negative reaction in you. Anything that hits you neutrally is not an issue with you; it is neither positive nor negative, so there isn't much new information to be gained from it. Conversely, the other reactions need to be noticed and further explored. When very positive or very negative feelings occur, these either signify strong preferences and dislikes or they signal lingering blocks, fears and false beliefs.

For example, if someone finds that she feels very positive about certain interactions, she has some information to add to her understanding of what makes her joyful. If others' behaviors are not fun or enjoyable, that is also helpful data to file away.

Feeling your buttons pushed by others reveals that you still hold beliefs that are not true, and these can be so deeply buried that they are sometimes not apparent until someone else's behavior rousts them. You now have a chance to clear those up.

Pushed Buttons, the Places That Go Bump, and Self Revelations

Extend the technique for restating untrue stuff into true stuff, from Chapter 6, to examine your inner self during interactions with others. Whenever there is a zing, hit or bump of an inner reaction that is not pleasant, it is a signal to check in (and remember that negative reactions to actual and appropriate stimuli are not the signal to watch for) with yourself and see where you stand relative to the Three Things.

You can notice if you still tell yourself stuff that isn't true, you aren't expressing yourself truthfully or you are still feeling responsible for people's responses. If you cannot tell what's wrong, also check the boundaries to make sure you are wholly responsible for yourself and half responsible for the connection.

If this doesn't clarify the problem, the source of the negative signal is residual untrue ideas and assumptions still lodged somewhere. These are affecting your ability to completely do the Three Things or maintain clear boundaries. You now know that whatever and wherever they are, these have to be dealt with because the negative indicator proves that these are definitely not true. Every time you take advantage of these opportunities to locate and remove hidden false notions, you will feel that much clearer, happier and healthier.

"But Hey Wait!" The smart reader says, *"If I have done the exercise for listening to my inner dialog and symphony, and cannot locate anything else in there that can be re-tuned, then the requirement to now find what I know I cannot find – hidden stuff – sounds like a ridiculous request, you knucklehead Margaret Ruth."*

Yes. Of course. But, one great facet of close relationships is this opportunity to further locate hidden bear-traps in the inner landscape. And I have a few more tricks up my proverbial psychic sleeve before we are done.

Spotting Your *Shoulds*

Life is like photography. We use the negative to develop.

– Swami Beyondananda

It is readily apparent that carrying around an internal list of *have-to*'s and *should*s is not only pretty typical, but also very unhealthy. I have noticed, and you may have too, that most people litter their life-instructions-to-self with *should*s and *must*s. In fact, and I believe psychologists are constantly battling this, these *should*s get so embedded in people's inner processors that finding them can take years. They have to be found though because they are always untrue and need to go. Otherwise, they create such monsters as stress, low self esteem, rigidity, panic, fear, anger, criticism and bad boundaries.

Even the spoken word is a problem in the English language. The word *should* has a deterministic, mechanistic, checklist-filling-in feel to it – when it's used to mean *must*. The word is an imperative and so feels like a brick or a heavy weight. The word is a command and so implies there is no choice.

One healthy practice you can acquire right away is to surgically remove *should* from all of your conversations with others and, especially, with your self. Take the time to discern more accurate phrases such as *I choose to, Some think it best to, One possibility is* and *I would prefer,* instead of *I should.* If you want to convey something that must be done, then only use the word *must.* Practicing this sharpens your self perception of when you are using the notion to diminish your self worth.

ISSUE BOX

When can I use it Margaret Ruth?
*When is using **should** OK? After all, it is a word in the dictionary.*

Should is a good word if it is used to imply uncertainty, probability, choice or conjecture. It is a nice word to use when it belongs with an "if" or a causation statement such as: "If the experiment works we should know in 10 minutes" or "If I want to record this, I should get a VCR" or "I should call her back, if I want to be considerate." No one should use *should* if saying it really means *must*.

When a person cannot uncover what is causing frustrations, upsets and bad feelings in a relationship, sometimes it helps to start spotting the *should*s. I have found that pockets of *should*s-that-seem-like-bedrock-facts create barriers to finding false assumptions in the psyche. *Should*s come in all sizes and can appear anywhere in a person's inner processes making them so very insidious, feel so true, and so very hard to unearth.

Here are a handful of examples of various difficult-to-spot *should*s that people carry around:

My spouse should be nice to me
My children should listen to me
I should be successful
People should read the paper
I should exercise
People should be considerate
My co-workers should not be so rude all the time like that
I should be attractive to others in the dating pool

I should get a degree
I should call my mother

All of these statements are false because in each case there is a
counter-example that can disprove it and/or the statement
reflects what is actually a choice. A person may have a high
preference for the stated things, but none of these are true statements as they stand.

For example, many people have an inclination for being
married to a nice person. However, there is no law that anyone's
partner has to be nice (*Obviously!* a couple of you are shouting).
The only mandatory item is what an individual prefers. A more
true statement than *My spouse should be nice* might be: *I have such
a strong preference to having a spouse who is usually nice that I choose
to only marry someone with that trait.*

(By the way, some of you, and you know who you are, can
keep the *I should call my mother* if you make it true by adding a
(highly) probable result such as: *I should call my mother or she will
be really upset with me.* It is now true because it indicates there is
a choice. An unattractive, dire and painful choice. Nevertheless,
a choice.)

Data Dump to Find the Nefarious Shoulds

Give yourself what you are aching to receive from others.

Give yourself what you seek from others, and you free them along with
yourself.

– Alan Cohen

Spotting *should*s is a very fast way to not only locate false statements, but also find unaddressed inner needs. Sometimes upset
occurs because we expect or need something from the other and
we think it's being withheld. The mirror of relationships, our
heightened reactions, allows us to discover where we are still
holding onto untrue beliefs and exactly which needs we yearn to

fill. When we discover what we need and are not getting, we are in very good shape. We now know exactly what to do for our self. It is foolproof.

I have a *Should Finder* that can work quite well if you cannot get to the bottom of what is bothering you about an interaction or a relationship issue. If you have considered everything we've covered and you are still carrying negative feelings around, this exercise might work for you. It works because it attempts to get past your thinking and analyzing parts and get you to muck around in the cellar of the self for a bit to see what you drag up.

Notice, though, whether or not the idea is overly frightening. Frankly nobody looks forward to this kind of excursion, but if the thought of it creates panic, don't do this exercise. Try other ways to uncover what is bothering you; for instance, the best recommendation is consulting the expertise of a counselor since an extraordinary fear of going too deep in yourself implies a need for solid professional support.

Should Finder Exercise Set Up

The *Should Finder* exercise has you go inside and dig up all and any anger, justifications and upset feelings stemming from an interaction to locate what exactly the other person needs to do to satisfy you or make you happy. When you know what you need the other to do to make you happy, then you know exactly what you need to do for yourself.

The time to do this is when you are distressed over how another handled his or her side of the relationship. Watch for fuming about another's treatment, ranting about some dereliction on that end, muttering curses about the other, replaying to everyone you can get to listen what she said, stomach upheavals, teeth clenched, nervous knots, inability to let go and other indicators of upset.

Just like the *Listening to Your Symphony* exercise, this one also requires privacy so find a closet or back porch where you will absolutely not be disturbed and no one is around. Have ready paper/pencil or a word processing page. Then you will need a mirror.

There are four steps:

1. Complete Venting and Data Dump

You have been injected with triple dose truth serum (which is why you need the privacy by the way) and the offender person is standing (the virtual version) in front of you. You are charged with expressing every last detail of what you think and feel about what that person said or did.

Write it down as best you can. Do not hold back. Many fairly healthy people do not want to write down the vile four letter words that are bubbling up from this deeply upset place because they know they would never express themselves like this. Forget that – you are sitting in a closet – just dump every bit of it.

Picture the person in front of you, feel the truth serum start working and go at it. Completely let it out.

2. Write Down What The Other Should Do So You Feel Better

At some point, switch what you are writing down to answer this question:

What should that person do to make you content, happy or at least not upset? Locate as many of these shoulds as you can.

Everything on this list will start with the phrase *You Should.* Examples are: *You should think about how I feel. You should promise never to do it again. You should give me the credit I deserve. You should be a better friend to me. You should love me enough.*

3. Take the List of *Shoulds* to the Bathroom Mirror

Take the list of what the other should do for you and stand in front of a mirror. Read them all out loud except they are all now stated with an *I Should* in front of them, replacing the *You Should*:

I should think about how I feel. I should promise never to do it again. I should give me the credit I deserve. I should be a better friend to me. I should love me enough.

4. Take a Moment to Understand What You Need to Do for Yourself and Yet Are Not Doing Right Now.

Finding these *shoulds*, in this way, will **always** reveal places where we are not taking care of ourselves well enough. Whatever lack we want others to fill is one that we have to fill ourselves and we know this because of the 100-0 Law.

If we are craving for the other person to be nicer to us, it is a certainty that we are not being nice enough to ourselves. If we don't feel loved enough by the other, it is a certainty that we do not love ourselves enough. As we know, no one can love us enough to *make* us feel loved; we have to feel it for ourselves first.

This last step confounds people for two reasons. First, many people will read an *I should* statement, such as *I should give me the credit I deserve,* and think, "Hey, I already handled that. I am perfectly self-affirming now so this exercise doesn't make sense!" However, if not getting enough credit is upsetting, then the self worth issue has *not* been entirely handled. The upset has to mean that the disturbed person still needed the others to bestow credit and when it did not appear to happen, in came the negative reaction.

The second difficulty is when an *I should* statement does not quite make sense, for instance: *I should promise never to do it again.* It seems strange but the statement contains information. It implies that the person does not want this to happen again – so that is a good piece of data to acknowledge. And it also implies that whatever the offender did, the person looking in the mirror needs to promise himself never to do that to others.

The remaining statements are more obvious. They suggest that someone is still not paying enough attention to her own feelings, still not treating herself perfectly well or loving herself enough. Her job is to commit to improving all these areas, *even if she thought she had already handled some of them.*

When you are venting and writing down everything that comes up around your upsetting feelings, there are a couple of things to watch for.

First, just because you want to kick the other in the shins, or otherwise hurt the other person, it does not mean you will do it or must do it. It is just a feeling that you are noticing. Second, if your wishing to be destructive towards another or yourself seems tempting to act on this is a red flag and means it is time to get to the counselor's office. Hurting yourself or others is a NO.

Case: Tyrell's Void

We always want someone else to change so that we will feel good. But has it ever struck you that even if your wife changes or your husband changes, what does that do to you? You're just as vulnerable as before; you're just as idiotic as before; you're just as asleep as before. You are the one who needs to change, who needs to take medicine.

– Anthony de Mello

Going deeper and finding places that are hurting from not getting needs met is very effective for finding stubbornly hidden beliefs, insecurities and fears.

Tyrell had been getting angry and hostile because his wife was spending so much time at the neighbor's; "Sharon and I have a really strong connection and I feel something is wrong when she pulls her energy away."

Sharon said, "I don't know why I like spending time with them; it's just that we get talking and gabbing and it is fun." They could not come to an understanding that pleased them both.

Tyrell knew his insecurities caused some of his angst so he tried the *Should Finder* exercise and wrote up his results.

"The first part took several hours. I pretended she was in front of me and that I had been injected with a truth serum and then wrote down everything I wanted to set her straight on, going very deep. I caught myself holding back because I started to access some extremely angry feelings and thoughts and these are things I would never tell anyone or say out loud. They were very mean. But I prompted myself to go there and let it all OUT like a purge of anger and hurt. It was all ok since I was just writing it down and no one was really listening.

"I finally got to what she should do so that I would feel better about everything. I wrote that she should recognize my value. She should care about me more than anyone. She should find me fun and interesting. She should listen to me and pay attention to my ideas. She shouldn't make me frightened of losing her. She should care about me being upset.

"I read them out loud in the mirror and switched them to the *I shoulds*: *I should find me interesting. I should listen to me and pay attention. I should recognize my value. I should care about me more than anyone. I shouldn't make myself frightened and I should care about me being upset.*

"Whew! These were hard to accept for many reasons. People aren't supposed to be fascinated with their selves and care more about themselves than others. It was hard to accept that I had to give myself what I wanted Sharon to give me. I found myself afraid that if I paid too much attention to me, that she would love me less. Honestly, this all was very scary. I understood them but couldn't see how I could do it all.

"I spent some time realizing where I needed to shore up my self concept. Looking at my shoulds indicated I had been holding beliefs that being married means only wanting to be with each other. I also tried to get clear of some remaining unhealthy notions about how married people are supposed to make each other happy and be responsible for the other's upsets. Since I was depending upon Sharon's love and attention to feel good, when she was away, feeling good went away, which clearly made me frantic! It was so obvious what was going on with me at that point, but it had taken getting really disturbed before I took the time to deal with it.

"So, it was in fact very true that *I should care about me being upset.*

"I recommitted to doing the Three Things in the relationship which meant trying to find and communicate the real me while allowing her choices. Doing all this felt frightening, but I also realized that my insecurities had taken the marriage to the brink already, so I was willing to change and become a more whole, self-affirming, self-valuing man.

"I became more conscious of what I was thinking. I began to focus on finding ways to make myself feel good. I began to generate some better and more interesting ideas for my life and for my work. In the end, it took weeks to get through the whole process, but it was worth it; the results were worth the time and effort it took towards mending our marriage, something I completely value."

Key Points Summary

Every relationship holds up a mirror for self discovery; following your feelings and reactions allows you to take advantage of this mirror.

Your heightened positive and negative feelings signify important preferences and point to places where you still have blocks, fears and false beliefs.

When something goes bump or a button gets pushed, it is a signal that you are still processing untrue beliefs, somewhere.

Check if you are completely doing the Three Things.

Spotting your shoulds is difficult but crucial because should-based beliefs are always false.

The exercise of *Should Finder* goes fairly deep and locates areas where you are not taking care of your needs and not making you your priority.

Exploring what is upsetting you about a relationship can also reveal hidden fears, false beliefs and personal insecurities that are otherwise difficult to locate. Once these are located, you can start to process them in a healthier manner.

Further Reading

Ageless Body, Timeless Mind by Deepak Chopra

Loving What Is by Byron Katie and Stephen Mitchell

Chapter 11

Pull it All Together – It Works

And the day came when the risk to remain tight in a bud was more painful than the risk it took to blossom. – Anais Nin

Derek didn't know how to react to his father's new approach. When Derek, 28, announced he had quit his job, he had steeled himself to withstand the standard disapproval lecture. But his father changed the dynamic and only asked "Why?" he did it. Derek just mumbled that he didn't want to talk about it.

Pulling everything together, I have made a nifty, handy, cheat sheet of what to go over when faced with frustration about an interaction. It summarizes the steps to check when you are sensing or feeling something is wrong with one of your relationships.

The best test and indicator that you are processing something that isn't true for you is when you notice some sort of negative reaction – a feeling, a sensation in your body, like a tension or an emotion, or something that doesn't feel neutral or positive.

Negative reactions associated with an actual stimulus in your environment are not the indicators to watch for. What we're talking about is tension, negative reactions or emotions that are clues to how you're feeling about something less tangible, maybe something that's just been said, or even something that's been left unanswered.

If you perceive a negative reaction associated with your interactions with other people, go over this check list to see if you can spot the problem and take advantage of this opportunity to gain more personal clarity and self-awareness.

Margaret Ruth's *Superconscious Relationships* Cheat Sheet

1) **The Good Working Assumption***: People are giving the best they have at this moment for this situation.*

2) **Check the Association**
   i) Involuntary, Professional, Impersonal? Non-adult? *Stop*
   ii) Voluntary? Social? Personal? *Keep going*
   iii) Something in-between? *Keep going*

3) **Check the Goal**
   i) Healthy, joyful, whole? *Keep going*
   ii) HJW not the goal? *Stop (wrong cheat sheet)*

4) **Check the Boundaries and EEE**
   i) 100% In charge of your inner self
   ii) 0% Others in charge of yours
   iii) 0% You in charge of theirs
   iv) 50% of the connection, no more/no less

5) **Check the Three Things**
   i) Thing 1: Am I fully aware of what is true for me?
   ii) Thing 2: Did I express my genuine self?
   ii) Thing 3: Am I clear of taking responsibility for what others choose?
   iv) Thing 3*: Did I meaningfully acknowledge the others' expression and complete the connection?

6) **Use the Mirror of Relationships** for More Self Awareness and Fine Tuning
   i) *Listen to Your Symphony*
   ii) *100% Accurate Test for What is True For You*
   iii) *Good Enough*
   iv) *Should Finder*

7) **Rinse and Repeat**

We know that our most emotionally charged relationships may be difficult but they also have the most potential to be transformative, and so next is a detailed and fairly comprehensive case that reflects one of those situations. The example is Derek's anger with his father and it demonstrates how Derek used his cheat sheet to drastically reduce antagonism and increase satisfaction with a problematic bond.

As you read on, try to think of any times when you've had a similar experience. As you think about this case compared to your life, remember that Derek can be any gender, any age and around 70-95% on the healthy, joyful, whole scale.

Derek's father in this scenario can be any gender or age and may represent any relationship that's important to you.

Also note that Derek's process worked for him because he was fairly emotionally and mentally healthy and the relationship he was working on did not fall into the abusive/destructive category, which demands immediate professional counseling.

The Case of Derek and His Father

> Man is made by his belief. As he believes, so he is.
>
> – Bhagavad-Gita

Derek was prepared for the usual confrontation with his father when he announced he had quit his job. When his father did something completely different, Derek froze. His dad only asked him: "Why did you quit?" For some reason, this new behavior threw Derek into emotional upheaval, which lasted into the next day.

He got out his cheat sheet the next night and began trying to isolate what was going on with him. *Ok,* he thought as he scanned the sheet, *first assume that this is the best my father has to offer for the situation and time.* He considered it for a moment. *Oh! Yes I do believe that,* he grimaced. *I don't sit around thinking he can do any better.*

He considered the other items. He thought his relationship with his father was fairly even, but he wasn't sure about the other points.

He checked the Three Things. He decided that he didn't know what was true for him, otherwise he would understand why he was more upset than usual. He decided that he had not expressed himself authentically, mostly because he had felt frozen and in avoidance during the previous day's interaction.

Being attached to how his father responded was also certain, because he knew a part of him continued craving approval. Derek deliberated the situation. *I see the problems, but have no idea how to fix them,* was the conclusion. *What else?* Derek mused.

He sat for a moment and realized he had skipped over the relationship goals because these seemed innocuous. But looking at them again, he found a part of him that was truly not comfortable envisioning a positive and happy connection to his father.

As a matter of fact, as he pondered such a radically new experience, there was a part of him that so identified with a Derek-defined-by-conflicts-with-his-father, that there was resistance to becoming a different Derek. He didn't know who he would be if he wasn't constantly at odds with his dad. *Great,* Derek thought, *I am hardly doing anything from my cheat sheet correctly.*

He sat down at the computer, placed his hands on the keyboard and closed his eyes. He began the *Listening to the Symphony* exercise, allowing himself to feel the inner turmoil, and started typing: *I have mixed feelings. Half of me is gut-busting angry and half of me is logically asking what this new approach is. Is it a real effort to finally understand me or just temporary?*

My angry part says: I am not you! I am me! You never approve of me. I can't do anything right – according to you. You never hear me. You never get me. You are always telling me what to do. Telling me to be more responsible! How can you SAY you love me and act like a complete jerk! Why didn't you even encourage me? Look at the good things I have done! Understand me! Respect me! Why can't you see me and love me just for who I am?

It became very hard for Derek to continue to write; hot tears of anguish from not being loved enough to be understood brimmed up so rapidly, he had use both hands for wiping them away. Finally the angry part was done raging, Derek drew a few breaths, and bravely asked *Ok, who wants to go next?*

He wrote: *My rational part wants to know what your new behaviors are designed to do. I want to know if this is some effort on your part to begin to understand me or whether it is temporary. Years of getting lectures makes me distrust this change. I risk spilling my inner self out to you only to have it corrected and denounced. My distrustful, logical part of me says that I do not want to spend much energy conducting a relationship if your reaction to my truth is the same as always. So, I don't know what to do.*

Derek stopped typing, leaned his head back and stared at the ceiling. Deeper questions flooded in about what he just wrote. *Why can't I just tell him how I feel and not care about his reactions? Am I depending upon Father to validate me? Do I want him to approve of me so much that I can't risk disappointment by being honest? Or do I hold back because it's a waste of time?*

He was still stuck, still distressed, having more questions than answers and not seeing how to untangle it all.

He looked at his cheat sheet again. Because he was still feeling bad, he reminded himself that somewhere in his psyche he was processing something that was not true for him. Maybe that is why he cannot find a clear way through his disarray. *Somewhere in all my jumbled thoughts and feelings I'm bumping against something that is actually false.*

He realized he had to find it or he would stay confused. He decided to try the *Should Finder* exercise since he was still feeling very upset and having real difficulties seeing what was wrong with him or what was at the bottom of his confusion.

Derek visualized his father in front of him and let himself go with everything he had. It was pretty straightforward because he had gotten pretty good at railing silently against his father over the years. This time though, he allowed himself to feel all of it and go as deep as he could. After all, that was the exercise requirement!

He easily generated a lengthy list of what his father should in order do for Derek to be happy with the relationship:

You should love me enough to approve of me.
You should listen to me!
You should understand me!
You should encourage me!
You should see me as I am, not as you want me to be.

He printed and took the list to the hallway mirror and, feeling a bit awkward, he read it out loud with the *I Should* substitutions for each.

Derek's discomfort doubled as this result clearly revealed the needs he was not meeting for himself; he was not listening to, encouraging, understanding or approving of himself enough. These realizations disturbed him because now he was looking at having to do all of it for himself, on behalf of himself. He had to understand himself enough to know what was right for himself and he had to fully encourage and approve of himself.

For some reason, staring at the unnerving reality that he wasn't treating himself very well, made him angry with his father all over again. *Why couldn't his father have shown him how to do all this while growing up? Why was he faced with the Herculean task of now having to find a way to love and approve of himself, without a role model, without much assistance?*

Terrific, Derek thought, *I was upset before, and now I am upset and intensely overwhelmed and ripped off because now I am taking it personally. I can't see how any of this is doing me any good other than finding out that I treat myself as badly as my father does.*

As he slumped back into his chair and stared at the *should* list in front of him, something clicked. He noticed that he thought it a fact that if a parent loves a child, then the parent understands and approves of that child. Mentally and emotionally examining this further, Derek realized that when his father failed to understand or approve of him, he felt unloved because of this bedrock, core belief. The idea of being unloved for those reasons produced a horrible sensation.

This caused quite a negative hit for Derek. He then KNEW that the assumption must be false. It had to be false because processing the belief made him feel miserable and therefore the 100% accurate indicator showed it was not true.

He started to feel a breakthrough. He wrote rapidly, *If it is not true that loving someone means accepting and understanding him, what is actually true? What is the link between love, understanding and approval? Can you love another without the other feelings?*

As Derek typed on, eyes blinking back hot tears, *Maybe the truth is that these do not have to be linked at all. Maybe the truth is that people can love even without approving; love and approval don't necessarily have to go together. Maybe it is the case that my father loves me the best he can without really understanding me or even approving of me.* He considered that.

That is amazing when I really look at it. If he does not approve of me and yet he STILL cares about me, the reason can only be because I am me, I'm his son, because I was born. If he doesn't approve of me, why else would he care?

The fact that someone loves me just for existing is incredible – massive – overwhelming. To my knowledge, he doesn't even seek to understand me or face our uncomfortable relationship. And yet – he still cares for me –the best he knows how – just because it's me.

The realization of this possibility buckles my knees. I feel like I need to gasp for air and my lungs hurt. It is so hard to imagine being cared about for no reason, not earning anything – loved despite disapproval – loved just for existing. Just because I Am.

He hardly knows the real me — he never asks — and yet he still attempts the Father role. He says he loves me and I've never believed him. With all that, it is quite possible that agreeing with me or understanding me wouldn't change his way of caring one bit.

The recognition that he was cared for, without being approved of or understood, sat more than just neutrally with Derek. It floored him and transformed him.

It crushed a series of false beliefs he'd held for years, such as: *I can't be myself and please my father, I need his approval, Not understanding me means he doesn't care.*

In the blanks where these old beliefs used to reside, new ideas rose up.

If love, understanding and approval are separate qualities, then Derek does not have to approve of everything Derek does in order to love himself, and he does not have to approve of everything his father does in order to love him. All of a sudden, sitting there and picturing a better relationship seemed easier: *We love each other despite not approving of each other's behavior.*

And he could at last envision saying honest statements in the future such as: "Dad, I would prefer that you rethink complaining as a way of expressing concern."

Waves of perfect relief cascaded throughout his whole being as he finally recognized what was really true. He thought: *And you know what, I do love him and he does love me and we may never understand or approve of each other.*

For Derek, finding the false belief and changing it into true statement was like a house of cards coming down. He would never again be as upset with his father as he had been; that part of their relationship was over. He faced a whole new set of challenges: understanding what was true for him, expressing himself authentically, finding out how to love and encourage himself, and above all, developing the new self-identity of a Derek who was not in perpetual conflict with his father.

Chapter 12

A Clear New Reality Plus Bonus
Refrigerator Door Material

Don't let yesterday use up too much of today. – Will Rogers

Writer Christy Karras came to love dating, and is even writing a book about it: "I think one of the reasons I came to like dating was that I had this long, dark night of the soul during my twenties where I totally freaked out and thought, What if I never get married? What if I never have children? WHAT IF I'M SINGLE MY WHOLE LIFE?"

"I think it was just after I broke up with a guy I thought was The One. I finally followed my fear through to its natural conclusion and really thought about what that would look like – and then I decided I had to be ok with it, or it would drive me nuts."

"So I thought of all the things that would actually be cool about being single. After a while, it began to seem pretty darn appealing. It also became the default. By making it the default when I looked at my future, I changed my whole outlook. When I eventually decided I wanted to be in a long-term relationship, it was a conscious decision."

In my view, Christy has already done for herself what my little book here recommends we all do. And it worked out very well for her. She found the parts of her that were knotted with fears of the future and clinging to falsehoods from the past. She was able to get those orchestra sections to start saying things that were actually true for her and playing a healthier, more harmonious personal tune. She then approached dating from a different perspective – the one where Christy was already a whole, complete person. She tells me it was at that point she started to love dating. I know her book about her experiences will be extra-ordinary.

You also have a future where you love your relationships. Understanding the five pieces of perfectly satisfying connections – your objective, the 100-0 Law and the Three Things – and allowing the mirror of relationship to show you the places still needing clean-up, will expedite your progress towards a healthy, joyful and whole you.

The happier you get, the happier you will be with your personal connections. You will get clearer every time you let the process work on your behalf.

Be Clear from Now On

Thought, in thinking about past pain or pleasure, gives a continuity to it, sustains and nourishes it. – Jiddu Krishnamurti

One thing I have learned to do, once I clear out a batch of old untrue beliefs, is keep the inner landscape that way – *clear*. If I don't keep it clear then allowing in new unhealthy gunk produces future bad gunk to bump into later, which will then require detection and removal, and the whole process seems like jogging in place on the treadmill. Terrific exercise, but I don't move forward and I don't get any fresh air. So, I watch what I add.

Even if you are still finding residual false notions and ideas, it is worth your attention to refuse to add any more too. Something you can do from now on is become conscious of how you are processing and retaining your current life experiences. Commit to only allowing healthy and helpful ideas through your filter. Let the unhelpful and untrue ones pass you by or pass through you without lodging in your system. There is a beneficial reason for this.

If you consciously or unconsciously activate old hurts and mistakes in a new relationship, there are now knots and wads of extra untrue stuff floating around the inner self. They are *un*true because these don't belong to the current outer reality; they are from a different time and hence a different you. Your current interactions WILL hit those, go bump, and you will get the negative impression, the signal of chewing on something that isn't true. We talked about dealing with those earlier and now we want to make sure you don't create any more of these messages, and thus have to deal with them at some future point.

If someone keeps allowing heartaches, disappointments, losses, sorrows and insecurities to be internally active daily – playing over and over like current news – and then continues to add to them, eventually that person will be weighed down emotionally, mentally and energetically. When you meet individuals who have allowed the system build-up to become excessive, you can almost sense a wall around them. They are energetically, psychically and, sometimes, literally *blocked*.

"NO!"

Picture yourself talking to someone whose inner landscape is so bricked over by fear, pain and sadness that she cannot generate any positive movement for herself. She sees no options for feeling happier.

From the window you can see sunshine and leafy trees. An elderly couple is walking by holding hands. A mini-van full of occupied child seats is passing by. Some teens are walking a lumbering, tail-wagging, beefy sort of dog (you know – the really cute kind). Inside you look around and see the pleasant living room with the family pictures and the cat toys littering the carpet.

Her keeping active a lifetime's worth of ingested disappointment and fear has created an inner reality badly misaligned with the outside reality you observe. The painful and unfortunate experiences of her life have created the walls, populated the landscape and painted over the windows of her life and world view. People diminishing their lives in this fashion actually exist.

Let's not do this to ourselves. We want to get unblocked and stay clear of sabotaging thoughts and beliefs.

Prevent New Stuff from Becoming Future Old Stuff:
Don't Swallow Chewing Gum

> Losing doesn't eat at me the way it used to. I just get ready for the next play, the next game, the next season. – Troy Aikman

We don't have to like everything and we don't have to think everything is wonderful. It is self-enriching though to gather ideas of what you like and do not like. You just cannot carry the negative stuff that happens around inside you as if it contains everyday treasures.

As you handle new experiences that are painful or disappointing, you need a way to insure these don't show up later and thus become the Old Hurts that cause the New (later) Baggage in your relationships. After a certain amount of time, crummy stuff that has happened needs to get processed, properly filtered and not allowed to infiltrate your day-to-day positive outlook. My favorite idea is to treat the filing of negative experiences like chewing gum wads.

When you have completed processing the pain/sad/fear

feelings caused by something that happened – and that processing could take awhile and require assistance to complete in a healthy manner – these feelings need to be handled so not to drift about in your psyche and wedge themselves as hurts and blocks and scars.

So, after you are finished chewing on them, they get wadded in the wrapper and filed in the correct receptacle, just like chewing gum. We know you can't leave the gum anywhere, you might sit on it. You can't throw gum on the sidewalk where you might step in it again. It is not good for you to swallow chewing gum; you don't know what it will do your system or how long it will lodge there.

Wrap up difficult or painful experiences by identifying what you have learned about your future choices. Ask yourself, what would I prefer to have or do the next time? What can I do better in the future to avoid feeling so badly? Then this newly gained and nicely wrapped information Wad is filed in the Wad receptacle labeled *Notes to Self on Future Choices*.

In other words, when the painful event is past, finish processing it cleanly by taking mental notes of what you learned and what you would rather have or do in your future; file these pro-active notes away until needed. Whereupon, the information Wad can be withdrawn and used productively in complete contrast to being destructively re-chewed and tasting horrible by making you feel lousy about your past.

Here is what the *Wads of Notes to Self* box might contain.

Wad Box: Notes to Self on Highly Preferred Future Choices

Dating unhealthy people leads to unhealthy relationships – don't do it again
It's more fun to have enough money, time and energy
Banging head on wall is UNPRODUCTIVE and expensive

If I'm not a good match for a job, either the job or I must change or there's no fit

Do not stand in front of moving cars

Wear a helmet

Forming tight and close bonds to unhealthy people is emotionally risky

If people don't ask for advice, I give it at my own risk.

I intend to be of continual assistance to the hungry and the poor

Fits of angry lashing out are only temporarily satisfying – don't do them

I'm going to be more understanding when others endure losses because it is so hard to recover

I want peace so much that I will do everything I can to promote it

Taking better care of myself will prevent feeling so ill again

Allowing myself to get railroaded by friends is bad for everyone concerned – stop

I promise myself to do better the next time

When you and I finish processing upsetting events, feelings and behaviors by figuring out what we learned and want to do better in the future, we are able to file the package away successfully. If tempted to revisit the upset, it will be harder to beat ourselves up with our mistakes and misfortunes if the memory wad is buried in a box of positive choices for minimizing future distress. This proper filing not only prevents us from harboring destructive self-talk, it is also more productive as it promotes even better choices for our future.

So, the chewing-gum-wad filing system works quite well.

My Answers to the Relationship Problems from Chapter 1

As promised, I have written up my very quick and bottom line answers to the relationship issues posed in Chapter 1. If you waited to read the entire book before getting here, you will be able to answer most of these by yourself. *I am not addressing you cheaters who peeked at this already, by the way.*

Read my bottom line responses below and then blend these with your own personality for your individual approach. It is your job to take my brief notes and add the fleshy, exciting individual details that reflect your unique consciousness

• *I work so hard at my relationships, why aren't they better?*
Healthy, joyful and whole relationships require your attention and effort to maintain; they do not require exhausting, draining toil. Make sure you know how to do each of the Three Things well, especially Thing 3. Acquire a sense of healthy and whole boundaries by fully handling your responsibilities and not accepting any that belong to the others.

• *I always date problem people – what is wrong with me?*
I know that you have issues when you tell me that you date people with issues. Check for which playground you are on. Get on a nicer one. Better yet –get on the HJW one. Then let's talk.

• *I always give and give and never seem to get it back.*
This is a violation of the boundaries and of EEE. Only you can take care of your inner landscape conditions. Others cannot do this for you and you cannot do this for others. Put your efforts back where they belong.

• *My mother-in-law makes me so mad – she doesn't appreciate me.*
Your mother-in-law has 0% control over and responsibility for how you react. It is not your mother-in-law's job to appreciate you. It is your job to appreciate what you do and it is your job to decide how close a connection you want to develop. If someone does not understand you, then why would you try to be very close? Do the Three Things as best you can, paying extra

attention to letting others be responsible for their own choices.

• Why can't I fit in with the others?

I don't want you to fit in with the others. I want you to treasure exactly who you are, exactly as you are. It is energetically incorrect to try to be something you are not, so this type of effort yields bad results such as exhaustion, stress, low self esteem and destructive ideas. The fact that you fret over not fitting in is a bad sign. Focus on getting to the HJW playground and forming connections by doing the Three Things.

• I always feel worn out by my co-workers' problems – should I quit my job?

Don't quit the job; quit breaking the 100-0 Law. Put a lovely semi-porous golden or pink bubble around you before entering the office and then FILTER. Do the *Prime You* visualization a lot, get specific with the kinds of information you will allow in, and be willing to test things – such as thoughts, beliefs, energies, feelings, opinions – before absorbing them.

• This relationship is a roller coaster – will it always be like this?

Yes. Unless both people get on the HJW playground. Only then will you have a HJW relationship. Make sure you understand that this means both – all two of you – everyone in the relationship – the totality of all involved in the connection. Remember, it takes two HJW people to make one HJW relationship (and there are no exceptions).

• All I want is for people to listen to me and they never do.

You are telling yourself some things that are not true, and you are not giving yourself some things that you want. In this case it is an easy catch – you are not listening to yourself. You are not paying attention to all your parts and all of your truth. And, now that you have cleverly used your negative feelings to help you get healthier, you can drop the untrue assumption that others need to listen to you in order for you to feel good.

• *My girlfriend never seems happy with me.*
Your girlfriend is not making herself happy. You will never be able to force her into happiness, no matter how nice or good or loving you are. If you want to be nice and good and loving, you do that because that is authentic for you. If you do them just to make her happy, you will both be miserable. Do your share of the Three Things, express your self honestly and allow her to be in solely in charge of her choices.

• *I have terrible fights with (_fill in the blank_) that never get resolved.*
You have several options. Try to use your reactions from this association to become more HJW than you are now. Carefully make sure you are doing the Three Things completely and halt any impulse to heal, fix and control the other. Your last option is to back away or drop your end of that involvement since it does not sound like too much fun.

• *I never feel like I have good friends.*
If you have read and understand what is in this particular book, start aiming to become the most HJW person you can be. Develop connections remembering the only Three Things necessary and you will not feel isolated for long. And remember, we are ALL rooting for you.

The Simple Psychic Truths

Quite a lot has been accomplished. The last chapter had a good summary cheat sheet for when you are feeling frustrated in a relationship. The following is the compendium of what we found out about superconscious relationships and perfectly satisfying connections.

The simple, metaphysical truths of fulfilling personal relationships are:

1. You are 100% responsible for the condition, content and conduct of your inner landscape. You are 0% responsible for other's inner realm and others are 0% responsible for yours.

2. Healthy, Joyful, Whole relationships exist and it takes two HJW people to make one HJW relationship.

3. There are only Three Things needed for authentic connections:
   Thing 1: Know What is True for You
   Thing 2: Express Yourself Truthfully
   Thing 3*: Choose Your Response to Others' Expressions

4. You have a 100% accurate inner mechanism that signals every time your inner processing hits upon an untrue belief, and that alert is a negative sensation (that cannot be traced to a nearby appropriate stimulus).

5. Because of this 100% accurate signal, heightened relationship reactions give you vital information about where you retain ideas that are not true for you; this mirror makes close relationships potent vehicles for self discovery and growth.

6. This brings us full circle to the universal requirement that the care and enrichment of your individual consciousness and life is crucial, important and the only

reason to be here. You are 100% in charge of that.

We also generated a nice set of relationship beliefs that are actually true versus prevalent myths. Here is the final list of these:

- *No one can complete another; however, love and support can be beneficial and appreciated.*
- *Healthy, joyful connections only take attention and effort; if there is arduous work involved and a relationship is constantly breaking down, that is not ok just because it is "normal."*
- *Relationships seem to thrive on cooperation, but someone who loves the authentic you will never ask you to compromise important parts of yourself.*
- *There are people who can be perfect mates, friends and buddies for you, and you can be perfect for them.*
- *Healthy, Joyful, Whole relationships are impossible to create under falsehoods and dishonesty.*
- *If someone doesn't get or isn't ok with your genuine self, do you have any business trying to have a close relationship with that person?*
- *It is not mandatory to be well-liked or have a lot of friends; some people enjoy that and some people don't care at all.*
- *The real key is to not find yourself by making people like you but rather make you like yourself, and then find like-minded people.*

Bonus Reading Material: Some of Margaret Ruth's Immutable Truths

Take off your hat to nothing known or unknown or to any man or number of men ...re-examine all you have been told at school or church or in any book, dismiss whatever insults your own soul, and your very flesh shall be a great poem. – Walt Whitman

I keep a running list of immutable truths and below is the portion relating to our discussion. These pithy statements about you and your relationships make good refrigerator door reading. Post, read, memorize.

MARGARET RUTH'S IMMUTABLE TRUTHS

Feeling Great is Better than Looking Great

Self Acceptance is Better than Other Acceptance

Self Love Leads to Other Love

I Have to Like Myself First, Then Find Like-Minded Friends

Inner Definitions of Happiness are Better than Others' Definitions of Success

There is no such thing as finally being good enough; there is only the process of living an authentic, enriched and fulfilled life

I am 100% responsible for the content, conduct and condition of my inner self.

I am 0% responsible for any other person's inner conditions

Everyone's opinions can define me unless I have a healthy sense of my Self and my boundaries

I need to get comfortable with the fact that I am complex because that condition isn't going to change anytime soon

All the Healthy, Joyful, Whole People are all running around –

dating, mating, relating with each other

The one thing I *can* control is how fast I get on the HJW playground

~

Let me know if you come up with some good ones of your own and I will add them to my list! And with that, we're done with *Superconscious Relationships: The Simple Psychic Truths of Perfectly Satisfying Connections.*

Key Points Summary

Commit to staying personally clear and refuse to allow unhelpful gunk build up by consciously processing your current and future experiences.

Commit to only allowing truthful, helpful and beneficial ideas past your filter by testing before ingesting.

Some people allow old hurts, fears and disappointments to cloud their current reality; building up excessive walls of these can make a person lose touch with outer reality.

Don't swallow the gum. A *Notes to Future Self* box, containing Wads of productive information about what you prefer to choose in the future, is a good filing system for upsetting experiences – once you are finished chewing on them.

I included my quick answers to the Chapter 1 relationship questions.

This chapter summed everything up with a compendium of the

simple metaphysical truths of perfectly satisfying connections and a final list of the true relationship statements we developed. A few of *Margaret Ruth's Immutable Truths* was also included for those who yearn for refrigerator door reading material.

Further Good Reads:

Oh the Places You'll Go! by Dr. Suess

The Artist's Way: A Spiritual Path to Higher Creativity by Julia Cameron

Chapter 13

Good-bye for Now

No man is an island entirely of itself; every man is a piece of the Continent, a part of the main…therefore never send to know for whom the bell tolls; it tolls for thee. – John Donne

You feeling the pleasure and joy of being alive is worth pursuing, if you haven't found it yet. In order to do this, you must first feel the excitement and thrill of being the perfectly unique individual that is living your life. When that happens, so many facets of your life will start feeling vibrant and interesting. Using the information that relationships give to you about you is a fabulous place to start – now that you know how to interpret the information correctly.

I did, however, make it more complicated than it could be. It could be a little simpler for some people. If you want superconscious relationships, you only need to realize the complete 100-0 law and commit to becoming as healthy, joyful and whole a person as possible. If you choose to become 100% self aware, self loving and self assured, and understand what is really true for you, then you are pretty much done.

If you decide to create a connection, it will automatically be healthy, joyful and whole. Relationships would be just fun icing on your party cake and make exciting vehicles to joyride towards expanded self knowledge and enrichment. For any of us not quite there yet, though, paying attention to the Three Things and using the mirror of relationships to become even happier and more confident is an extremely effective way to evolve and grow.

I'll see you on the playground.

You'll Be Fine

Thank you for reading this. Your comments and questions are the only way I learn what needs to get addressed, so keep them coming. I invite every single one of you to join me and comment on the Facebook Margaret Ruth page for my next book on dating and mating, the current working title of which is: *Only Four Things Are Necessary for Enduring, Healthy, Joyful and Whole Partnerships*. Good title, eh? That, as you can imagine, is a terribly popular topic and I will need your input.

It's me, Margaret Ruth here, with the last ISSUE BOX
There may be some small leftover arguments or complaints hovering out there about what we have been discussing. I am going to ignore them now.

Our book's modeling of the only Three Things necessary is structurally sound and proves to be true if 1) Your goal is satisfying, authentic and healthy connections and 2) you at least partially accept the 100% - 0 Law.

The 100-0 insight laid the foundation for a relationship framework that gives you what you truly desire. The model is complete and compelling; I cannot find a place where it needs fixing, adjusting, shoring up or adding to or decorating or mucking with....

The nice thing though is that a person does not even have to believe the 100% - 0% Law for this book to be helpful. All one has to do is entertain the possibility it is true, and start closely observing him or herself, other people and the world around to test its validity.

However, for those of you who would like to speed up the process, you can just accept what is really true about

---

you and your inner processes, and leap immediately from there by adopting the Three Things.

Either way – it will all work. And you will continue to feel better about you and your relationship experiences. And everything else we hear out there that seeks to add *complications*, and *what-abouts*, and *you-also-need-thats*, are either just relationship-icings, helpful hints and lovely decorative elements OR are actually not true at all when it comes to forming authentic and perfectly satisfying connections.

And now you know how to test for yourself what is really true for you and are set to filter and sort the outer stuff that might come at you. Keep just the stuff that helps you transition to where you want to be – Healthy, Joyful, Whole – and ignore the rest.

You'll be just fine.

Come and see me sometime – I would like to hear your story. MR

Thank-yous, Appreciations and Acknowledgments

My heartfelt appreciation goes to clients, students, readers, listeners, and Facebook contributors for the responses, questions, stories and input. Sincerely I say that nothing happens without you.

Thank you also to everyone at O Books and John Hunt Publishing for all the help and contributions to this book.

Some very fine thinkers contributed every step of the way with ideas, words, suggestions or support. Thank you very much for your contributions (in random order): Rose Olds, Beverly Josephson, Christian McCrea, Tyrell Forrest, Guthrie Goeglein, Daniel Griffin, Greta DeJong, Cramer Hall, Matthew Howcroft, Sharalyn Howcroft, Heather Johnson, Greg Near, Patty Rayman, Cathy Coleman, Christy Karras, Allen Seviers, Mark Felder, Sharon Webb, Kyle J. Oman, Jerri Webb.

Thank you Kerry, Bill and Gina, Richie, and especially the listeners of the world class radio morning show *Radio from Hell*, which obviously attracts world class listeners. If this book proves useful to anyone, it is because of our work together on KXRK FM 96.3, in the USA, for almost a decade. This particular book is my anthem to you all.

My thanks to Jake O'Donnell and Jim O'Donnell for equipping this book's manuscript preparation editor so she could work with email downloads, word processing and Skype calling.

Because, after all, nothing says *I Love You* more than being forced to proof Chapter 3 five times, thank you to the creative talents in my family. Thank you to Joyce Laird, F. Judson Laird III, F. Judson Laird IV, Jim Hensler, and Laird Hensler.

BOOKS

O is a symbol of the world, of oneness and unity. In different cultures it also means the "eye," symbolizing knowledge and insight. We aim to publish books that are accessible, constructive and that challenge accepted opinion, both that of academia and the "moral majority."

Our books are available in all good English language bookstores worldwide. If you don't see the book on the shelves ask the bookstore to order it for you, quoting the ISBN number and title. Alternatively you can order online (all major online retail sites carry our titles) or contact the distributor in the relevant country, listed on the copyright page.

See our website **www.o-books.net** for a full list of over 500 titles, growing by 100 a year.

And tune in to myspiritradio.com for our book review radio show, hosted by June-Elleni Laine, where you can listen to the authors discussing their books.

mySpiritRadio